Relati◉nship READY

MOVING FROM #RelationshipGoals TO
A WISE FOUNDATION FOR Relational Greatness

LeANZAR STOCKLEY

Soulciety01

COLLABORATIVE ALLIANCE
FOR RELATIONAL WELLNESS

To my grandparents Harold and Ella Winters

Rest in the presence of God our Source and Creator. To know Love is not only to know God, but also to have been the descendants of the two of you and seeing Love manifest and emanate from your being.

CONTENTS

PREFACE

My life's work has been dedicated to humans and their relationships – even though I don't consider myself to be one of them. Ok, I am kidding already and it's not even a good 5 pages into the book yet. I guess I am human too. There, did that make you more comfortable?

Anyway, as I was saying, it seems like my life has been and will be dedicated to human relationships. This being our relationship with the Creator and with one another. I personally sense that this is an extremely meaningful dedication and truly speaks to the reason we are even experiencing life in this way (this way being a spirit-soul, having the human experience).

Prior to being a Relationality Specialist, I served in the Christian church as a Worship Leader. Prior to that, I was a dude that grew up in a world that always seemed weird to me. These "human people" seemed a bit strange to me, particularly in how they dealt and related to one another. Needless to say, I had to attend therapy as a child because the monsters I saw in my nightmares were actually not monsters at all, they were people who simply mistreated other people. Early in childhood, my attention had been drawn toward human interactions and how we do life together. To some degree I felt out of place. Yet, as my life has progressed, I have realized that I belong. For as long as I can remember, I've had a personal relationship with God (yes, even before being indoctrinated with religious beliefs). Accompanying that "personal" relationship came conversations that, from the outside looking in, folks would have thought I was strange. Ok, they did think I was strange (*LOL*).

Anyway, I would clearly hear that some of the ways we related as humans was a bit skewed and often a misstep. It was as if I could see things before they happened, or I knew some things without "learning" them.

Fast forward, I have later come to know and accept that I was experiencing what we might call "the gift of the word of wisdom". Someone once referred to me as perspicacious. After I explained to them that I didn't really sweat that much, I decided to look it up and find out its real meaning. Pretty much it meant having a ready insight into and understanding of things. I guess there was some truth to this, which leads me to why I am mentioning any of this in the first place.

While I in no way want to present or make a claim that I have the monopoly on truth (as a distant friend of mine phrased it in a wonderful social media post), or that I have all the answers, I do want to offer what I sense and believe to be words of wisdom for people seeking to get into or enhance a "significant other" type of relationship. I cannot count the times that as a Relationality Specialist that I have been faced with family, friends and strangers talking about their unsuccessful partnering relationships. The amount of exes' people have had and the age-old comments that they fell in love with the wrong person, are too numerous to count.

Needless to say, as I have pondered these situations, I would be remiss to withhold what I sense and hear in regard to these things. I am concerned that we have so many failed relationships. I guess if you are a spiritualist, you would probably say they aren't failed relationships, they are just lessons, or transitions. Well, even if that is the case, there is a responsibility and wisdom that I think we need

to align to that will help us more than it will harm us as we romantically couple together.

This book really is just a highlight of a few things that I have identified as wise virtues of alignment in being prepared and ready for relationships period, however this book is geared specifically to the romantic infused relationships. Again, the wisdom outlined is specific to these individuals, but not exclusive to them. Whether you are currently "in the market" for a relationship of romance, already taken, or just want to add to your wholeness as a single person, there is something in this book for you.

As you navigate through this book, please keep an open heart and mind. Understand that I am not presenting as an expert, but instead as a friend just having a meaningful conversation with you. Of course, the points in this book are not the totality of the matter; however, I do believe they offer some helpful insights as you begin to "be all you can be" in the army. *Ooops*, I mean, be all you can be in your relationship.

INTRODUCTION

#RELATIONSHIPGOALS

I mean ... look at them. All cuddle buddied up on a cold and starry night. Feeding one another so adorably at the sushi restaurant. Making little love tap marks on one another's canvas while enjoying date night at the Paint and Sip. Who cares how the painting looked? They themselves were the perfect picture. Listen, not a week goes by without them posting themselves, just loving on one another with the salutation hashtag in all caps, #BAE. Hmph! Oh, and the last one of them lying in bed, waking up in the morning together like a couple that has no worries in the world, with their bank account in the positive, really was over the top. Ugh, they are just the perfect couple. I mean ... I am not jealous; I am just anxious. As much as I would like to not play into the fairytale, I can't help it. I can't help but react to the post, taking 999 likes, loves and wows to 1003. Hey, I reacted from my main account and my aliases; don't judge me. Ok, and I can't help but lay down my pride and comment like the other fans ... #relationshipgoals!

Does the above commentary about the perfect couple sound familiar? Perhaps even sounds just like you. For the sake of saving face, we won't say that it sounds like you. Let's just say it sounds like someone you know. It is no foreign feign that we all desire to have great relationships. For some, the mere appearance of a great relationship will suffice. Hey, the old folk used to say, fake it 'til you make it.

More than just having a great relationship, it's difficult for many of us to not want to go a step further into having a perfect relationship. You know, the ones that look like they should win the compatible couple of the year award. Now that ... that's really what we are being sold when we take our desire feedings from the vast majority of the social media posts and outside view of the relationships we think others are adorably having.

We won't play any games here. For many of us who actually desire to be in a coupled (or thrupled) relationship, it's hard to not see some couples and think, "Wow, I would love to have a relationship like that." If we are being honest, sometimes we just want to be able to say, "Wow, I would love to have a relationship ... period; one that I can use the good ole' #BAE for." Let me say this, there is nothing wrong with wanting to get you a #bae; just know that in the Danish language bae means "poop." And, "bye" in the Icelandic language. So much for your sweetheart of choice (*inside laugh*). Hmmm ... maybe that is why so many have a #bae this month and a #LovingMe, #CleansingFromToxicEnergy, #WorkingOnMe salutation next month. Ah, who knows?

Sorry for the sidebar; let's get back to the topic at hand. Regardless of the desire, there seems to be a search – or prayer for those who want to wait on the Lord to deliver, for the right person to come along to carry this desire into the realm of breakthrough. That's just a nice way of saying the realm of heavenly orgasms and tickly toes. Ok, I have no idea what tickly toes means, but I bet you know what I am getting at. Point is, there is no shortage of people looking and waiting for "the one."

The reality is, there are some things we must understand and embrace as we seek to have our desire for a partner that's worth others admiring and tagging with the trending #relationshipgoals. While we all know there is no such thing – in our perceived lifetime, as a perfect relationship, we must embrace the idea and reality that we can actually have a PERFECT relationship. Yes, I know what I just said, and no it was not a typo. For those of you who didn't catch what just happened here, let me explain. There are two ways in which we can use the term perfect. One use of the word suggests that something is totally without flaw or blemish; it is perfect. My first use of the word perfect basically means, without error.

Another use of the word PERFECT is something that is characterized with qualities for being mature and equipped with what it takes to be wise, resilient and thriving. Given this second use of the word perfect, please know, you can have a PERFECT relationship.

Some people like to call this the perfect, imperfect relationship. Whatever you want to call it is fine. Just know that as we delve deeper, what will really matter is the heart and spirit you embrace in order to qualify the hashtags you follow, post or are honored by. If you are into that sort of thing.

Furthermore, it is extremely important to note and remember that the idea of finding the right person has a couple elements to it as well. First of all (does it sound like I am fussing ... well I am.... NOT), being the right person must precede finding the right person. Even considering this, we must truly explore for ourselves what that even really means? What is a "right person?"

Personally, I often find the phrase to be a bit laced with self-righteousness and potential self-absorption, but hey, that's just me. I do understand what most people mean when they use such phrasing; so, for that reason alone, I will use it for conversational flow.

Anyway, moving on from my personal rant, let's get back to the point.

Aside from being the right person, it must also be understood that finding the right person is so much more than just finding someone that checks off all the romantic desires on your list. Finding the right person is more about readiness than it is about romance. Yes, it may be a romance infused relationship that you want, however, please know that for most long-term relationships, romance alone is a weak foundation to build upon.

Despite how eager we are to be in a relationship, being ready for one is a totally different stance. I will say this again for the people in the back. Many people are eager for a relationship, but not ready. It goes without saying that to enter into a relationship you are expecting to qualify as something soulfully meaningful, you must be ready not just eager. As a matter of fact, if you enter into it eager but not ready, you will potentially disappoint and be disappointed; perhaps even if the sex is good ... oops I meant, even if the romance and chemistry is good.

True relational compatibility isn't necessarily about who serves your romantic ego. It's ultimately about collaborating maturely with the spirit of one another's being. Being ready for a relationship is about maturity and even a sense of purity. It's about engaging with one another in ways that cause our Love nature to rise to the occasion versus just operating on the auto pilot and inebriation of being "in love," romantically.

If you've read my book entitled *Relationality: Consciously Aligning To Our Divine Relational Worth*, you know what I am talking about. If you haven't read it ... well, shame on you. Go read it!

In this book, we are going to delve into what it really means to be relationship ready. Understand, I am not offering you some quick fix formula for masking your true self or manipulating and intimidating others in an attempt to land the relationship. What I am sharing here is just a few nuggets of wisdom that has been downloaded in me. I am confident and hopeful that as you read this book, you will find your spiritual intelligence unlocking, submerging you in the necessary relational wisdom you need to soar in readiness for the relationship your soul desires.

In this, I am hopefully just serving as a presence and voice of Love for you in helping you thrive as your authentic being. I am rooting for you to show up in a way that not only positions you for your own good, but also for the good of others; to the point in which you can say to them, #iAmLove4u and therefore qualify the honor of #relationshipgoals.

CHAPTER R

RELATIONAL PHILOSOPHY

It might seem minor to understand how reason's play a part in why people get into partnership type relationships; however, we can't be naïve in realizing that the obvious of wanting a partner may be layered with many additional layers. It is not uncommon in my work and practice as a Relationality Specialist to hear a plethora of different reasons people have listed for why they are with a person. In all reality, sometimes there can be as many listed reasons as there are people. Generally, however, many of us have been cultured and accustomed to giving similar answers.

Many answers are often seemingly based in pleasure. The good ole' phrases like, "I want a cuddle buddy (as I was told at one time in my life by someone). Let's just say, they seemed to want more than a cuddle buddy. Or either I have the wrong idea of what a cuddle buddy really is. Maybe it too is coded like the nice, sweet innocent phrase "Netflix-n-Chill." Anyway, there are also many people who come right out and say, they want a sex partner, or "f buddy." You all know I couldn't say the real word ... I am a righteous man, damn it (LOL). Hey, Damn is in the bible. That f word ain't! Well, depending on how you read it. Ok, point is, there are many pleasure-based reasons people give for wanting to be in a relationship.

There are those who are simply honest with it and say, "hey, I just don't want to be by myself." While many experts and spiritual teachers will side eye skeptically to this answer, I believe it carries a lot of value and weight. If we are honest (and human), we must realize that we weren't designed to be alone. It is completely and perfectly – in its own right, not just normal, but also natural to not want to be alone. We are relational beings that were designed and created for meaningful relationships.

Granted, being with others doesn't always have to mean we have deemed those people our romantic partners or significant others as many like to call them. However, the overall principle remains that we usually desire to have someone that we are close to. Even those who identify as asexual are not counted out of this number. Just because they are asexual, doesn't mean they are aromantic ... and deeper than that, it doesn't mean they are arelational. A lack of desire for sex, is not a lack of desire for intimacy, close connections or a partner.

I know that is hard for sexuals to comprehend; however, maybe it helps to remember that everyone seeking a partner, isn't necessarily seeking them for romance or sexual engagement. Chances are, many of us could potentially have a hard time understanding reasons for relationships that aren't quite our own. Nonetheless, let's approach this as if we are all in this together because ... well, ultimately, we are.

The point is, there is something deeply ingrained in our being that is drawn to a close relationship with another person. For those of you who are itching to rebut this statement, let me interject and note that I am aware that there are some people who for whatever reason have no identified desire for, blockages, disorders hindering, or drawbacks from relationships. That would mean that much of what I write in this book may not be for those people. Now that that is out of the way, let me focus on those who this is for.

The deep longing inside us to be in close relationships with another human being is natural and part of our design. So, when people answer with simply not wanting to be alone, we must allow validation for that answer. Of course, we want people to explore a bit deeper and hope that their answer isn't coming from a place of self avoidance; but overall, the answer is coming from a place of health and balance.

Other answers I have heard are things like, wanting someone to share a life with or needing someone to start a family with. In all reality, we have our reasons; many of which are valid. But when I talk about being relationship R.E.A.D.Y. I am suggesting that we delve deeper. Not just giving primary or surface answers, but giving more conscious, core intention anchors. Intention in relationality is crucially important. It often attracts and bonds to like energies.

Again, I am not necessarily aiming to give you the answers as much as I am aiming to be a catalyst and support in the unlocking of your own spiritual intelligence regarding these things. As it relates to the reason element of relationships, I want to present a few of what I call, WOWs (words of wisdom) and wise questions, to kick you off in exploration which may make your preparation for a partnership – or refreshment in your current one, more meaningful. Want to hear it? Well here we go!

What's Your Relational Philosophy?

When we are talking about reasons – as stated above, what I am really asking you about is not the surface "duhs" that are obvious for people in establishing a relationship, but instead, what is the guiding core intention that you have identified as to the importance of your relationality and relationships overall. What is your relational philosophy? What is really guiding your motives, desires and engagements? Whether you have identified it or not, you have a relational philosophy. There is something that governs not only why you engage relationships, but also how you engage and disengage them.

For many people, this may sound too deep, or complicating the matter. However, when I look at the divorce rate, how quickly #bae changes to #DoingMe, the obsession with unfriending, unfollowing and cutting one another off, I can't help but think the matter needs to be addressed. This is a deeply important question that needs to be answered and consciously employed as it might just save us some unnecessary heartbreak or heart hardening.

Your relational philosophy plays a huge governing part in how you see relationships. Perhaps how you experience them as well. It can be the very thing that determines whether you are obsessed with finding grounds for togetherness and marriage or grounds for separation and divorce. This might sound very silly, but believe it or not, many people are operating in relationships from a negative or lower consciousness. Although the vast majority of people who want to be in a relationship – and don't necessarily enter into one only to break up a short time later, the philosophy informing them might be the culprit for their loss. Many people aren't aware that they are actually relationship negative, instead of being relationship positive in consciousness.

If we're being informed by a philosophy that seeks grounds for separation, versus grounds for moving into one another, we will constantly find ourselves in a cycle of breakups. This cycle has the potential to lead us to hardness of the heart and having mentalities of individualism which in turn can lead to pure functioning as a narcissist. This pattern flow may seem extreme to some of you; but look around, our world is filled with people who somehow *"got the way they got"*. Perhaps even you have noticed a change in yourself and how you deal with and see relationships because of past experience; namely, failed relationships and negative experiences.

These things don't just happen because humans are incompatible or because we have found the "wrong person." They happen because in so many words, we aren't ready. We haven't established and centered ourselves in a relational philosophy that lends itself toward successful relationships. I don't just mean wishing and hoping and manipulating for a successful relationship. I mean truly establishing and planting ourselves in a relational philosophy that ultimately is not just our moral code for dealing with others, but also our code of ethics.

You see, our relational philosophy is in essence, our governor. This doesn't mean that others will always respond accordingly; however, it does mean that we have a center to return to or ground us when they don't. Without a solid and energetically positive relational philosophy, healing from breaches in our relationships might just be nothing more than cover ups. To truly heal, we must have a philosophy or wise realignment to Love.

When our philosophy is negatively charged, we run the risk of sabotaging ourselves over and over again. The sad part is, most times, we move on thinking we are fine and have learned some valuable lessons. But again, if the lesson you learned only made you more skeptical, more guarded, a harder heart and less trusting, then that was not healing. That was simply ... "moving on."

Adopt A Spiritually Scientific Philosophy

I have summed my relational philosophy up in basically five words. It not only informs how I aim to relate to others, but it also informs how I deal with and care for myself. Not only that, but my philosophy has deep roots in spirituality and human biology. My relational philosophy is pretty much encompassed in the words "I am Love for you," aka for those of you that have followed me or seen one of my brands, #iAmLove4u accompanied by the relationality symbol. You can find that on the cover of this book as well as my book *Relationality*. In all actuality, it has become my mark that you can likely find anywhere you find me.

The outer circle with the three dots represents the African Ubuntu Philosophy which in simple terms says, "I am because we are." It is a recognition of oneness and how we all are interconnected, deriving from the same source and responsible for one another's well-being. Inside the circle you will find the OM/AUM symbol. It simply represents the various stages of consciousness. For me, it is the most important reminder to consciously live Love and my authentic being. Abstractly surrounding the OM symbol is a heart. We all traditionally know the heart to represent Love. You see, in that symbol alone – for me, lives and breathes my relational philosophy. It lends itself to my reason for relationships. It informs how I relate to others and my core purpose for any relationship I engage, entertain or indulge.

Biologically speaking, we are wired for Love. Research has shown and correlated Love with wellness and thriving. As I explained in the book *Relationality*, our brains are wired for Love. To the point that when activated properly, our whole body responds in a thriving manner. When absent, we deteriorate faster, experience depression and other mental setbacks, and have limited resilience for sickness and disease. Remaining in (and as) Love, is for lack of better words, crucial to the human experience.

I personally feel that we all should embrace the philosophy I have. But again, what does your spiritual intelligence reveal for you. I'm pretty sure if it is truly your spiritual wisdom, it will lend toward the same; however, this is something you want to explore to emanate, not just shrug your shoulders and accept in an attempt to imitate. What relational wisdom guides your relationality and relationships with others? When you have fully established and anchored yourself in this, you are positioning yourself in alignment toward readiness.

Write the Vision, Make It Plain?

Where there is no vision, the people perish. Maybe that is what plagues a lot of relationships as well – a lack of vision or visioning. When you think about it, have you ever been in a relationship or seen one that just seemed to be on autopilot or perhaps seemed to not be "going anywhere?" Or worse ... going somewhere that is potentially deeply harmful? I know I have.

Now before I get too deep into this, let me clarify some things. A lot of the language we use in regard to relationships and one another tends to get lost in translation for me or end up being presented in a way that I feel leaves the fragile human mind to process inappropriately. When I say I have seen relationships that seem to be on autopilot or it seems to not be going anywhere, I am not really implying that there is "somewhere" to go. A lot of times when we use or hear this terminology, we are thinking the relationship needs to progress through the socially constructed stages of courting to marriage, etc. I am not talking about that. Other times, the thought may be that going somewhere in the relationships means advancing in reaching some business goal or becoming what many consider a power couple; again, based on some social construct or status quo. I am not talking about any of that.

My use of the words "going anywhere" is more about consciousness and being for one another the rock and anchor needed in the accountability structure of a relationship. We will talk more about this later. In the meantime, in between time, I want to highlight this particular topic of going somewhere as it relates to developing a vision for your relationship.

Now, for those of you who are currently in relationship, this is something that would be best done together as you are currently in the trenches and wouldn't want to create a relationship vision without the actual person you are in relationship with. That would be rude and borderline ... rude. Yes, I know I said rude twice. That just means think about it twice.

Now for those of you wonderful souls who are in the preparation stage of a relationship (meaning, getting yourself positioned), the visioning is something that you are doing alone and in so many words, calling things that be not as though they were. Either way, having a clear vision for the relationships is important and can be a guide used in not only having an accompanying support for your relational philosophy, but also having a go to for guidance on how to develop as an individual or couple when the time arises. Or when you feel yourself slipping out of line.

As a Certified Relationship Workshop Facilitator, one of the resources I use in doing relationship workshops is material from the Enlightened Relationships Workbook, published by Transformation Publishing. The workshops using this material highlights four P's that are important to remember when creating a relationship vision. However, before we go into the four P's, let's talk about what a relationship vision ultimately looks like. It's not very difficult at all – at least you should try to make it fairly simple.

A relationship vision is like your vision board (for those of you who do them), except it's solely for relationships. You can do this for any relationship, however right now we are specifically talking about preparing yourself for your partner. Your relationship vision is where you, to the best of your ability, write out the details of your ideal relationship. This is not just a list of deal breakers and what you don't want. I suggest that you take cues from your overall relational philosophy. Use this opportunity to tap into your spiritual intelligence to access the necessary wisdom for making this vision. It is important that your vision is viewed as a spiritual document, not just your ego tripping. That might be hard for some of you (smile).

Now, let's brief the four P's really quick. Present Tense, Personal Perspective, Positive Language, Passionate. Ok, just a bunch of words, right? Well, let's break it down. When writing your vision for your relationships, you will want to keep the verbiage in the PRESENT TENSE. You are writing as if it is now. There is something very interesting about our brains. It processes things in a way that causes you to look for those things. If everything you put in your brain is future tense, then your brain will process it as something that will happen or come one day.

Remember, earlier I stated that visioning is like calling things that may not have manifested yet, as though they are, right now. If you write your vision in present tense, as if it is now, you are training your brain to embrace and create that reality now. Of course, there may be some setbacks or obstacles; however, you don't want your brain to be informed by the obstacles. You want your brain to be informed by the spirit of your vision.

Another important writing point for visioning is to keep it on the up and up! Use POSITIVE LANGUAGE. Again, you are not writing a list of what you don't want. You are writing about what you do see yourself being, doing and having. If your focus is on not wanting something, guess what you might have a plethora of? Yep ... something you don't want.

A lot of our language is subliminally relationship negative. Stop, think and watch how often you speak of relationships and/or other people. Are you able to identify potentially how negative you are in regard to them? You know, the talk about having trust issues – "people always this or that." The commentary about having to protect yourself and fight for you. Where is all of this coming from? A lot of this talk is actually fueled by negativity. I am not saying that it is invalid. However, while visioning for your relationship, it doesn't serve you and causes you to engage negative energy although you are seeking something awesome and amazing.

Here I want to interject the PASSIONATE part of the four P's. I think this is a perfect time to incorporate this element because we are talking about the engaged energy. I am sure you will most likely be passionate about your relationship. So why not be passionate about your vision. When you approach this process with passion, you are filling it with your whole, authentic, spiritually intelligent energy and wisdom. While you may be aware of negative things that you don't want in your relationship, that energy can be transformed into positives because you are envisioning a life free of such pain. Free in the sense that you – to the best of your ability, neither create it nor continue to experience it. Be excited that the vision you are creating will be realized and actualized in your lifetime.

The last aspect of writing your vision is PERSONAL PERSPECTIVE. I am sure you have heard it one hundred times over in therapy or any other self-development setting. Use I statements! In this case, because we are talking about relationships, you will be using both I and or We statements. It is important to remember that a relationship is not all about you. It is inclusive of another person. The use of I (depending on what stage of visioning you are in) is not to be narcissistic, instead it is to be included and accountable to what the vision outlines. It speaks to how you plan to show up and do your part in creating a great relationship.

Using "we," just further positions you and helps you to realize that you are a team working toward a common goal. It speaks not to compromise, but instead to a collaboration that will yield a beautiful and authentic creation. Basically, what I am saying is take your time to be inclusive with your vision and speak about it from a personal perspective. The relationship you want is not the relationship your neighbor has. While the qualities might be the same, this is not a copycat or mimic game. This is the engaging partnership of your soul and the soul of your Lover. It is important and, in some ways, unique to what the two of you create together.

So, let's bring this all together. You want to speak in present tense, use positive language, be passionate and personal. These are great characteristics for the vision, but the content of the vision is where it is fleshed out. When writing your vision, you want to try and include every area that you can think encompasses a relationship. Don't just write about how romantic you want things to be. Don't be that shallow. Your soul is much deeper than that. You are much more than a few dozen roses and long walks on the beach at sunset.

When thinking about the areas to include in your vision, you want to think about intimacy, communication, what you want your family or team to look like, what goals you want to accomplish together, perhaps what home life should be like, spiritual partnership, how you want to resolve hard times, etc. Come on, you are worthy of Love and so is the person you are in relationship with or preparing for. You want your vision to be reflective of such divine relational worth. Don't shortchange it nor fill it with ego. That would be belittling and just plain dumb! Fill your vision with points of wisdom, not wisdumb!

Built Up In Love

Now hear me out. Whether you are in a relationship or in preparation for one, you have to remember that that is what you are building ... a relationship. I felt the need to return to this just for the people in the back. A relationship is not all about you alone. It is about an *us*, a *we*, a *y'all*. Part of establishing reason for a relationship is truly to dive into purpose. This is both individual identification as well as collective.

Having a clear sense of who you are is super key to having a sense of who we can be together when we merge and integrate within the relationship. This is not a rant about self-love and how you have to fully know your purpose before getting into a relationship with other people. Reality is, sometimes pieces of our purpose are hard to understand because others will always be the piece we are not understanding or embracing. Whoa! That was deep. *Selah*!

We do have to have a healthy level of understanding of who we are; however, I sense that the ultimate reality of who we are is connected. None of us are here to be alone or all one. Don't get me wrong, we are to be whole. But we also must understand that one whole plus one whole only makes another whole. Go pray about it because I don't have too many more ways to try to explain what the heck I am saying. If you were in the spirit, you would know what I am saying. My goodness (smile)!

No, seriously, all I am saying is that we do have to have a sense of purpose for ourselves, however when we really delve deep into our purpose, we will usually find that it is connected to others and therefore the wholeness and purpose we bring, along with the wholeness and purpose they bring, will only launch us into the greater whole. Often, there is a plaguing confusion and frustration in people having a sense of purpose. A slight word of wisdom here is this. One of the first and primary steps in gaining a sense of purpose is to simply be present. Recently, I was carrying a friend of mine in my heart and communion with God. During this time, I heard the words to tell her to not focus on an assignment as it related to her purpose, but instead to focus on being present in alignment with the Divine and who she is as a being. The words of wisdom went on to say, "when you are confused, be present. When you are frustrated, be present. When you are engaged with others, be present. When you are in solitude be present." It boiled down to practicing presence. This might sound very unrelated, but the practice of presence has deep wisdom in helping you align to and understand our purpose, both individually and collectively. Chew on that gum for a while, blow some bubbles but most importantly, make sure your breath is gets fresh before you proceed.

When we approach our relationships this way, we are building. When we do not approach our relationships this way, we are demolishing and instead of making whole, we are making holes.

I feel the need to say that this also doesn't mean that we won't come into relationships with some baggage, some hurt, some areas that need healing, etc. Oh, for as long as humans exist on this planet, we will be carrying some stuff with us. The ultimate aim is to be mature in the carrying; and embracing some of the other elements of being relationship R.E.A.D.Y. that we are getting ready to dive into.

Everyone, every day, will not always be at 100%. This is a potential reason we have a desire for and embracing of being in a relationship. A function of relationship is support. We are sabotaging the house if we don't go in understanding that we need help and have to help one another build. It is important to remember that we are each built up in Love as each person does his or her part. The ultimate reality is we are building a relationship of (and in) Love.

The Lover of Wisdom-Philosophy

The word philosophy is actually made up of two Greek words; *philein sophia*. This translates as lover of wisdom. My charge in this element of being relationship ready is that you be a lover of wisdom and more importantly, a Lover in wisdom. When you are clear, or as clear as one can be on reasons or reasoning for relationships, you are better positioned to be ready for one. This says you have established a core, a center and aim of intention to live by as it relates to yourself and others.

If it is a true Love relationship you are seeking, this is not something you want to ignore or just count lightly. The reality is, humans live by a philosophy of some sort. Wouldn't you want the one you live by to be one that causes not just yourself, but also the one you Love or will be Loving to thrive? Afterall, Love is ultimately about thriving, not surviving. It seems like wisdom to live by philosophy that embraces a we mentality. Pure reasons for our relationships are crucial to the relationship success. Look at it this way. When your reason, intention and philosophy is pure, you have set the stage for a positive, healthy and divine relationship. Both you and your chosen partner are definitely, #WorthIt."

CHAPTER E

Have you ever heard the phrase, "do unto others as you would have them do unto you?' Good, glad you've heard of it, but this ain't what we are about to talk about! Ha ... Gotcha! We are going to talk about something similar and some related elements. It seems that treating others the way we would like to be treated is somewhat of a universal belief spanning across many different religions, societal ideologies and adopted moral codes.

I too, feel this is extremely important and a very great spiritual practice. However, I also sense that it is important to dive deep into another realm of nature within us. Empathy – and by extension, emotional intelligence. You see, emotional intelligence is basically the capacity to be aware of, control and express your emotions, as well as the practice of interpersonal skills and handling relationships fairly and empathically.

Taking a closer look, we see two things at work here. One is the ability to know and express your own emotions. But when we draw on the part which calls for us to handle relationships with others empathically, we are engaged in a deep and meaningful reality that speaks to our nature as relational beings. We are drawn into not just knowing our own emotions, but we also develop the ability to understand and share the emotions or feelings of others.

Granted, some people are better at this than others, however I sense that the essence of this virtue lies within all of us. It is an element of our divine nature. Yes, even though we are human. You mustn't forget that being human is still spiritual. While it is a distinction, I do not believe that it is necessarily separate from being integrated with the Spirit of life. Anyway, empathy is something that is ultimately a core virtue that we can and need to develop if we are expecting to be successful in the relationships we engage. Without this quality of emotional intelligence, we are likely to really mess things up and potentially screw other people up in the process.

Transforming Experience Into Intelligence

Recently, I was in a conversation with a friend and we were in discussion about his relationship and processing his desires versus the desires of his significant other. Of course, as with many conversations regarding couples, the topic of sex, drugs and rock & roll came up. Oh wait, my bad. Scratch the drugs and rock & roll part. Well ... let me think for a minute, we might be able to use that whole phrase. Standby, we'll see if it comes up.

Anyway, the topic of sex came up in terms on one person's drive being high while the others is not as active. While this was a specific conversation between my friend and I, this in no ways an uncommon topic of conversation with any number of individuals, couples and groups I provide coaching for. What a great joy it is when you and the person you are in relations with are on the same page, at the same time, the same drive and the same high (pun intended, see, there is the drugs part). When you and your partner are both experiencing the high of being in love and completely ready to rock and roll (see there it is) at any time of the day, perhaps even multiple times a day, oh what a glorious concert to be enjoyed.

The challenge arises when music isn't in sync. When one person wants a walk on the beach and the other wants a roll in the sheets. Now we have a different kind of friction going on. It then becomes the survival of the fittest or the one who can throw the biggest tantrum for not getting what they want – the way they want it. Here is where the clash begins and the questions of compatibility, etc., come in. Of course, the reference here is concerning sex, however, regardless of the topic, the concept is the same. One person is on page five, while the other person hasn't even opened the book yet.

During this conversation, something very mature came out the mouth of my friend. Now, while the words physically came out of his mouth, I believe it was flowing from his heart. It is true in this case that out of the abundance of the heart the mouth speaks. In his own words, I heard my friend saying that he deeply Loved his partner and had no desire to not be in the relationship. His feelings had not changed. The only thing that had changed was his drive for sex. Additionally, the lack of drive for sex, was in no way a lack of desire for his significant other. He went on to say that he is torn only because he knows that for his partner, it could seem like rejection. My friend stated very clearly, "I know what it feels like to be or feel rejected."

Perfect (mature)! Here is something deeply important. He was able to use his experience not to play against his significant other, but instead to empathize with his significant other. Folks, you see, we all have very similar experiences when it comes to emotions and feelings. We all have experience with wanting something. We have experiences with feeling rejected or less than worthy. We all have had experience with pain of some sort. While the details of these circumstances may vary from person to person, the overall feeling itself is common to humanity.

We get in trouble when we dismiss the feeling just because the situation might not be the same as ours. In a sense, pain is pain, desire is desire, rejection is rejection. The details surrounding it shouldn't cause us to belittle or disregard the feeling others have. Yes, there are things that seem minor, which to us do not merit the feeling of rejection; however, it's not really up to us to determine the intensity of one's feelings. We will talk about this a bit more in a moment.

The main thing here is to understand that we have the ability be it from mirror neurons in our body or contemplation, to empathize with others. We can identify with the feelings we have and know how we felt when placed in certain situations. This positions us to really take into account how we could be contributing to how others might feel. When we do this, we are now faced with the call of Love to not want our significant others to go through the same feelings. We are in this very moment given the opportunity to Love them, collaborate with them, support them, be patient with the, etc. I mean, the list could go on and on. Bottom line is you are transforming your experience into empathy boosting virtue.

At Least Know They're Human

There are times that may seem a bit more difficult to really understand how another person may feel. It's funny because this is not just in what we call negative feelings but can also be in what we consider to be positive feelings. As I mentioned above, sometimes we try to assign the intensity rate to other's experiences. We compare our experiences to determine the intensity someone should be feeling. This is rude and dangerous. You might think your feelings from losing your grandmother are more intense than your partner's (or anyone's for that matter) feelings of losing his or her job. This can get us in trouble. Again, we have to understand that regardless of the details, the presence of grief is on duty. Period. A lesson in empathy is not to measure the intensity, it's to simply be present in the knowing and sharing of feelings.

To use another real-life story here, I will tell you about a conversation I had with another friend. She talked about how difficult it is to recognize her own light and to understand why people would Love her. She questioned if perhaps her children Loved her because she was their mom – alluding to a socially forced kind of Love. She also questioned if her husband Loved her out of obligation. Words of wisdom began to surface during this conversation. I immediately felt impressed to say to my friend that trying to figure out why they Loved her is ok; however, it could also drive her crazy. What really is important in that moment wasn't to assign her own judgments to why they Loved her; instead it was to simply honor the fact that they Loved her.

You see, there are times when we can't identify exactly why someone feels how they feel, but we must simply honor and know that they feel. We might not be able to assign proper judgment to the depths of their Love, but we must embrace the reality that they do – just like you, Love. Part of empathy and emotional intelligence is this very thing. It is embracing that fact that when we can't necessarily identify with the exact feeling another person has, we can identify with the human reality that they do feel something. Understanding those feelings might have to come in deep conversation with them. But just because we don't understand it initially or identify with it initially, doesn't mean their feelings should be invalidated.

There are things that I truly don't understand the desire for; however, that is in terms of details. But one thing I do know is what it is like to have a desire. That becomes the point of empathy and emotional intelligence in dealing with the people in my life. No, I have not mastered it completely, but it definitely is a point of contact. There are times when I simply don't know what a person is feeling, but I do know and sense that they feel.

You see, we have to realize that feeling is a human capacity and at the heart of our nature. This is when we recognize that we are more alike than we are different. Even though we like to highlight our differences (because of that part of us that likes to be exclusive, unique and special), and spotlight our distinctions from the rest of the world, we have to realize that we are all still human, all still have relationship at our natures core, and all have feelings; sometimes ones that simply aren't understood by other humans. This too we all can generally identify with.

I See You

As we align and develop in our emotional intelligence and empathy virtues, we begin to expand its concepts into more areas of our lives as well as show up in the world more effectively as relational beings. Being sharp empathetically and having keen emotional intelligence plays a huge role in how authentic we are and our ability to connect. Now remember, a portion of emotional intelligence is being aware, in control, and expressing your emotions appropriately. In being ready for relationships, we really have to sharpen this. You definitely need to be able to recognize your emotions and take the necessary steps to process them, prioritize them, place them and present them.

Your feelings are often like temperature gauges. They are indicators and signals that alert us to different happenings within us and responses to stimuli of some sort. Relationally speaking, you are much better off if you are aware and able to express yourself in honesty – one to yourself and two, to your relational partners. Please do not neglect this. Do your best to sit with yourself, examine yourself and process appropriate ways to embrace, share and even advocate for yourself if need be. I am not talking about snapping on people and giving clap backs about what you deserve. However, I am talking about humbly understanding that you are worthy of Love just like those you give Love to.

In collaboration with being aware of your own emotions, practice being aware of others. Granted, at times, this requires communication, openness and mutual disclosure, but nonetheless, make it a priority. Your soul and the soul of your significant other will thank you for it. You see, as you go deeper into your virtue of empathy, it literally becomes the breeding ground for so much of your relational health. The virtue of empathy simply says, "I see you." It is basically your ability to connect, be authentically present and cultivates the space for your significant other to feel comfortable doing the same.

It is more than just saying, "I hear you." Truth is, some people talk to be heard – and that's fine. But what we really want is to be felt. No, I am not talking about being felt up ... although that can be nice too. But, as I was saying, we don't just talk to talk and hear that we have been physically heard. We really want to hear the words, "I feel you." We want people to as much as possible be able to identify with what it feels like to be as we are. This is not saying that we have some evil desire for people to be in the same pain we might feel. I mean, at least for some of us. It is just saying that we really want people to understand the magnitude or intensity of where we are; that way, there is a greater sense of oneness, sharing, maybe even responsiveness or seriousness taken. Now, please don't confuse empathy with sympathy. It is not a matter of just feeling sorry for someone. It's being able to identify with how they feel. When you truly understand in this way, you are moved differently, you sort of step into their shoes. When we really and truly feel one another and have a basic understanding of one another, we are able to tackle our issues much better.

In so many words, empathy is like an unspoken form of communication. As a matter of fact, it is a boost to our communication. Personally, I consider it to be sort of like a spiritual voice ... a spirit-soul communication skill.

We all want this. Why deprive ourselves of it? Yes, it causes us to be open and many times that openness can be frightening; but nonetheless, it is crucial to us being authentic to who we really are and living up to the design in which we are made. Being an empathetic master (used lightly but rightly) is key to our readiness for relationships. It sets us on a path to not only put our ego's in check, but also our ill entitlements and potential mistreatment, misuse and abuse of one another.

If the kind of relationship you are wanting is one that is marked with true Love and care, empathy is not a mere amenity, it is a necessity. Just imagine what your relationship will look like when you have entered a mutually ready relationship with someone that has done or is doing the same work you are doing. The kind of work that is not just done for yourself, but that is done because you want to give the greatest Love possible to the person you are with.

Empathy is so powerful. Don't make the mistake of thinking that emotional intelligence and all that jazz is just about you and how you deal with you. You see, most things relationally charges are not all about the self. We, as human beings aren't even created to be so independent and individualistic. We are all part of a greater whole. As stated earlier, we all are working together being built up in Love. This doesn't take away from the personal work; it simply qualifies it and draws the personal work into the greater whole that includes the significant other and beyond that, your close family and friends – so on so forth.

What makes your empathically strong or emotionally intelligent is not just your ability to see yourself. It's all about seeing us. Seeing what environments stimulate or depress our emotions. You see, being empathetic just strengthens your relationship in ways unimaginable and supports the authentic flow of one another's core. I am rambling about this because it is sort of like an energy center that is undervalued or just viewed as a nice moral accessory to have. No folks, it is powerful beyond measure and opens the door to realigning not just you and your relationship, but humanity as a whole to its pure design. And oh, what an intelligent design it is!

When you align to the empathic virtue within you, position yourself to give your relationship what it needs to thrive. You see, it's a grace within you that will cause grace to exude from you to those you are in relationship with. You don't have to try and muster it up. I feel the need to say that. Again, the virtues I am sharing in this book are already within us. Many of them just need to be uncovered, dusted off, polished and presented. They are already fruit that grow on the tree of our core being. You don't have to fake like you have empathy. That will backfire at some point. You simply have to uncover the eyes of your heart and say peek-a-boo, I see you!

CHAPTER A

ACCOUNTABLE PARTNERING

Listen, I don't know why the Creator created us as relational beings. Perhaps it was some form of a bet between light and darkness. Or maybe it was some Hunger Games type sport to see how quickly we'd kill each other in efforts to save our own lives. I am kidding! The reality, however, is that we are relational beings. Period. Even though at times it seems like we are obsessed with trying to live separate, act separate and be separate. The truth that will break us before we break it is that we are connected. As a matter of fact (even though you didn't ask for my senses), I personally sense that when the Creator God did his whole human creation "thing", the mind wasn't individuals but instead collectives that are distinct, yet extensions of the same Source, Spirit, Energy or Consciousness. It sure does seem to line up, both spiritually and scientifically. But meh, what do I know?

Now, taking into account that we are relational beings, drawn to one another, connected, conforming, comforted and even irritated by one another, speaks volumes. One huge part of being relationship ready is to accept the fact that we are relational; connected. We have to embrace the fact that our greatest reality of self happens within the realm of relationship with one another. For this reason, we must stand in accountability. Yes ... the "A" word – accountability.

I know, I know, not many people want to have to be held accountable. This is perhaps one reason many people do their very best to avoid having to be accountable to anyone other than themselves. We want to be our own truth and live our own truth, right? Well, get this. What if there is a bigger picture? A bigger picture reflective of the connected relationship and core essence of our being that makes us relational. Is seems that no matter how much we try, we can't get away from it. Even if we chose to isolate ourselves, could it be that in some way we still are affecting those who once knew us? Yeh, I know you don't think you are that popular, but despite the contests you might have lost, you are still important. Even if you can't identify how, the fact that you exist, counts you in the number of humanity and worth it. I don't want you to lose sight of this worth because not only is it truth, but it also one of the reasons we all must be accountable.

The bigger picture is that because we are all relational and affected by one another, there is reason and need for use to live as such. We must take into account the presence and affect we have with others. We have to take into account that while we can live in freedom, that freedom doesn't mean that we live any kind of way or do whatever the hell we want to do just because we feel we can. The reality is that our freedom shouldn't be a bondage for others to have to suffer through and survive. We have to be accountable in how we show up in this joint. For this reason alone, kindness, gentleness, peace, patience, and all other virtues make sense. If life was just you alone, you wouldn't even have to take a bath if you didn't want to. You could sit in your own funk for as long as you wanted. But, since you don't live here alone, go wash yo' tail. And while you're at it, brush yo' teeth too! That's Love. Thanks.

Although I am making light of this situation, please know that in all reality, if you are not willing to be accountable, you are not ready or suiting yourself for a coupling partnership. You have to take this concept and apply it to every area of your life. Relational accountability takes into account the physical, mental, emotional, financial, spiritual, etc. It's the depths of placing your life in accountability not only to our design, but also to our chosen relationships.

Your Higher You

Considering this talk about accountability, contemplate the idea that one of the primary functions for relationships is centered around authenticity and support for us living in sync with our highest sense of being. You see, we have grown more accustomed to relationship only being for our pleasure and enjoyment. We generally as a collective do not think of them as design, help, and something crucial to our overall health. I get it though, it's not really fun to think about them in that capacity. However, when we discount them to mere accessories for pleasure, we abandon something very powerful within ourselves and one another. I know that is not popular talk these days. Even amongst spirituals, there seems to be a huge obsession with the self and not being attached to things or people. Without going too deep into this, I want to say, we must be careful that our spiritual stance doesn't draw us away from the fact that we are still designed as relational beings. As a matter of fact, our spiritual stance is often questionable when it leads us into being relationship negative. That doesn't seem like the guidance of the Great Spirit at all. But again, meh, what do I know – other than what I know?

As I stated above, a function of relationship is to support you as your higher being, and for you to support others in them living as their higher being. This is where we are really built up in Love and truly serve one another. Here is where we feed one another with life giving fruit of the spirit. Here is where we provide for one another a garden filled with not just tasty fruit, but also beauty, peace and the harmony of soothing songs. This is also the place where we provide for one another the opportunity for tending to the garden, pruning what needs to be pruned, and watering that which needs to be watered.

If our only idea and thought for being in a close relationship with someone is for pleasure, we run the potential of missing the fullness and wholeness of life. We run the risk of feeding our desires, while our design goes to the pits. We take the chance of losing the true depths of our essence thereby shallowing the experience of what it means to be fully present, fully human, truly seen, honored, Loved and cared for.

Placing yourself and holding yourself in accountability to a suitable helper is one of the most mature things you can do. It is a display of your willingness to not only be vulnerable, but also your willingness to align and be all that you can be in the army. Oh, my bad, my mind drifted again to childhood memories of the United States Army commercial. Anyway, being in relationship with a significant other is a form of planting yourself and giving yourself the ground, safety, security and support for living out the fullness of your destiny.

Again, this is not just about you – nor is it about control or being controlled. Being in relationship means that you too are willing to be the suitable helper for your relational partner to be supported in their higher being. The whole idea of man not being made to be alone (all one), is that we would have support in our being. It's to have someone to bounce things off and process things with so we aren't left to ourselves. Left to ourselves, we can be a mess.

The term suitable helper denotes not just one to tickle your fancy, but one created to be equal with. One to stand alongside you.

Not one subject to you, but equal in power, presence, protection and provision. Being in accountability isn't about hierarchy, being submissive or dominant one – as we tend to take it. The word suitable helper actually translates as lifesaver. Yep, life saver. The people you are in relationship with should be in some way, saving, preserving and supporting your life. "Zar, you mean to tell me Jesus isn't the only savior I am supposed to have?" Glad you *snidefully* (yep made up that word) asked. To that, my bold answer is ... contrary to religions, popular, societal and some spiritual beliefs ... NO. There is something essentially saving of one another coded in all of our being.

This really is why wisdom is important, why living in this virtue is important, why being pure toward one another is important and why truly Loving one another is important. We are essentially in this together. Sure, we all make mistakes and miss the mark. It goes without saying that we mess up sometimes and even have moments where it seems we are failing one another. This is all the more reason we need support in being our higher being. Being accountable to one another to live from the spirit of our being is the thriving energy we need. It helps us to help ourselves as a human race. When we can truly say, "I am because we are," we are putting a blessing on our relationships and lives that are second to none. We are aligning to the Creator's design. What better way to be blessed than to be aligned to what we were created for? Come on folks, the accountability thing is not about taking something away from us. It is ultimately about delivering something to us that is deeply crucial to our thriving.

When we abandon this important element of being relationship ready, we only set our loved ones up to be hurt. We set ourselves up to be junkies – relational junkies. We leave ourselves to only be being fed by the drug-like inducing highs of being "in love." We will find ourselves, jumping from relationship to relationship; potentially from one bed to the next. Experimenting with people's lives instead of truly graduating to experiencing true unconditional Love or the greatness that comes in actually being Love for one another. In short, we leave ourselves open to be a beast instead of a priest that properly stewards and hold sacred this gift of life, Love and relationships. Significant other relationships are designed in a way to be the space you need to really be that spiritual being. They have a way of getting to you (and into you) in a way other relationship may not. They are a spiritual partnership. It makes sense, this is likely one of your most intimate relationships and sees you at both your best and worst.

Breeding Ground of Spiritual Intelligence

Since we are talking about being a priest of sorts. Let's look at this from a wisdom standpoint. You aren't being accountable just because you want a relationship with someone. Thereby using the claim of accountability for manipulation or enticement. You are being accountable because in the grand scheme of things, it is the spiritually intelligent thing to do.

If I am not mistaken, the term "spiritual intelligence" was coined by a lady by the name of Danah Zohar; however, there is a definition by Cindy Wigglesworth – author of SQ21, that I like to refer to when thinking about the term. She defines spiritual intelligence as "the ability to act with wisdom and compassion, while maintaining inner and outer peace, regardless of the circumstances."

The better you are aligned to your divineness, the better you are toward experiencing what it means to be whole. In turn, you are contributing to a greater good – that is the wholeness of another. You are essentially acting in wisdom and compassion – very important to a relationship. You are doing your part in creating a world of Love, justice, peace, etc. Your relationship reaps the benefits of a field that brings forth fruit in every season.

I generally don't talk a lot about spiritual growth because I understand it more in the sense of alignment to who we already are and the fact that the spirit of our being is already full and mature. I sense more that what we mean when we say spiritual growth is more like getting better at integrating the rest of our life with the spirit of our being. It's the recognition that all is in oneness. For me, it's really just the unlocking or revealing of our spiritual intelligence.

Embracing accountability is the breeding ground of spiritual intelligence. It says that we aren't choosing selfishness. It says we are recognizing a bigger picture. It says we are willing to Love to the best of our ability. It actually says, we are willing to have a great relationship. It also says that you are willing to be seen and know for who you really are. When we provide this type of space for one another and nurture this intelligence in one another, we better position ourselves to be at peace within ourselves and with each other. Accountability, especially as it relates to spiritual intelligence, leads you to taking off any masks you may be wearing. It is awesome because when done in Loving space, not only can you and your partner be realized for who you both are, but it kills the need to defend or protect any false images of yourselves that have been constructed. Being in safe accountability with one another has the potential to put you at ease, which in turn helps you feel less and less threatened. Yes, I said threatened. You might be surprised to know how many people actually feel threatened in their relationships. This sometimes is the real truth at the heart of all this "protect" your energy and toxic people talk. You might be surprised how many people enter relationships guarded – not because they are just afraid to be hurt, but because they are afraid to lose themselves. Being in accountability actually calls you to being yourself; not losing it.

Now, while all of this sounds too deep and spiritual, please know that all these things aligned, doesn't mean that the fun, pleasure and enjoyment will be taken away. As a matter of fact, when you process it correctly, it gives you grounds for more fun, pleasure and enjoyment. It might actually increase your fun, but I am not going to tell you how. I will let you figure that out for yourself. All I will say is ... rock and roll!

Wholeness gives happiness greater meaning. Pleasure, fun, enjoyment and happiness – without the support of wholeness is nothing more than having a good taco on Taco Tuesday. It was good eating, but the heartburn afterward ... well that's another story. Anyway, accountability is not a restriction for yourself; it is a commitment to releasing your full self. It requires you to tap into the depths of all that you are and bring it to the surface so that your contribution to the planet is one that is marked by the character of God etched on your soul, manifest as YOU. It's actually pretty dope.

Let's face it, if you really Love the people in your life (in this case your significant other), I am sure you want them to have the best that life can offer them. Why not live up to being one of the best things that life has to offer. Why not hold them accountable (not by force), to be the same for you. As I stated before, both you and they are worth this type of wisdom and compassion.

Heck, if we really want to be real, while we don't do the personals of our relationships as a show for other people, we could take into consideration that there is a generation of people watching and taking cues from us. Being relationship ready and embracing the self-control and virtue of planting yourself in accountability that brings out your best essence, is teaching the next generation about their own worth, value and showing them what real Love looks like. Again, although your aim is not for show, you at least have played your part in qualifying the hashtags for the generation of people who follow that sort of thing. Why not give that following a truly great relationship to want to be like versus all the ones that aren't really what they photograph as?

When it's all said and done, if you aren't in a place where you are ready to be accountable, the Loving things for you to do might be to refrain from potentially putting someone through the torture of having to partner with you in that way. At best, let them in on the fact that you aren't interested in true accountability and allow them to decide for themselves what steps are wise to take. What I am saying is, at least be accountable enough to say you don't want to be held accountable. Hmmm ... I guess that is still me saying, be accountable, huh? Well, I couldn't help it. See! I was accountable enough to you to tell you that I couldn't help but tell you to be accountable. I am practicing in living from my own higher being as I tell you it's a wise thing to do as well. Give me a break here. LOL.

CHAPTER D

DEVOTIONAL CREED

Devotion is a word that I personally believe is reserved for another human being. Something you give to another spirit being, another living soul, another life. Ah, you get the point. I sense that is a much stronger word than commitment. This means that the decisions that I make and the steps that I take are taken into account, my union and my oneness with the other person(s) in my life. So, when I make changes in my life, be it for bettering myself, choosing to live from my higher being, careers, living environments, etc., there is another person in mind. I know this is not embraced very well; but usually that is either pain, fear or mistrust talking. The spirit being (who we really are essentially) understands this idea as "home."

Honestly, many of our resistances to wisdom is potentially fearful parts of our personality peeking its head up for self-preservation. I get it – trust me, but when Devotion is done in the Love and wisdom, it is pure and undefiled. Does this mean it blocks you from ever being hurt, disappointed or done wrong by someone? Of course not. The only things that shield that is death.

As we talk about this relational quality and wisdom of devotion, I need you to be brave. It's extremely easy to fall into the trap of fear that whispers in your ear saying, "you'll lose yourself." That is one of the biggest crocks of you know what. Being devoted is not about losing anything. It is about being fully present and showing up in all your fullness. We really have to stop falling for all this rhetoric that draws us farther and farther away from living in oneness with one another.

We can continue to complain about how horrible the world is and how much we can't trust people. But the reality is, if we don't take the stance and position that we will live differently than what is commonly adopted, our complaints will continue to rule and reign. In addition to that, they will continue to cause us to be on the same side of discord that we are complaining about.

People talk about Love, loyalty, trust, and all that, but I wonder if we have been afraid to truly employ any of this ourselves. We will talk about this a bit more later; however, are we truly embodying these qualities or are they just something we want people to give to us? Truth be told, if our loyalty is based on someone else's loyalty to us, we can't truly say we "are" loyal, we can only say we have engaged in loyal behavior or was held by a time-limited loyalty contract. Behavior and being are not always the same thing.

I was in a relationship that sadly ended. A buddy of mine made the statement, "now you are free, you don't have to ever lose yourself in a relationship again." Immediately I had to correct my friend. You see, I was not lost at all. I was very present. This doesn't mean I didn't make mistakes or have moments where I was absent minded regarding my partner. However, overall, I was devoted to the relationship. Devotion wasn't a matter of losing myself in the relationship. Actually, in so many words, I found more of myself. I will say this again … devotion is not about losing yourself; it is about being yourself. If you sense and believe that you have any worth, you will be serious about what you bring to the relationship; not just about what the relationship can bring to you or how deeply it can stroke your ego. It's all about you showing up as authentic, Loving and supporting as possible. When you identify this in yourself, I promise you, you position yourself to serve your relationship – and yourself, with something so powerful.

My friend suggested that I had lost myself because I was still deeply in Love with the person and grieving the relational shift – even after finding out about infidelity going on. I had to explain that my stance in the relationship and the Love I had was not based on the person being faithful or Loving me back. It was because it's who I am. You see, ultimately, my behavior was driven by who I identify as; not by what others are necessarily giving. Now, hear me out. I am not saying that people are obligated to stay in disharmonious relationships. The point I am making right now is much bigger than the details of your relationship. It's more about the authenticity of your being, being made present.

Here's the thing, virtues must first be identified within as core elements, capabilities and natures to our being, before they become the doing of our being. Yes, I get it. Sometimes, we act on automatic. Sometimes we act with ill motives. Sometimes, fear driven motives. I get it – we don't seem to always be pulling our actions from the very core spirit of our being. However, this doesn't mean that it doesn't exist. This is what it really means to do something from your heart. You have found the light in yourself and decided to allow it to shine past all the other obstacles, walls, or temptations that would try to hold it back. Doing something from your heart means you have identified that something pure resides there; and that whatever that is needs to be manifested in the reality of your life or toward others. You realize that it is in you; so, you simply live it out.

What I want you to see in this is that in being relationship ready, you have to not just have devotion, but BE devoted ... be the devotion. This requires that you embody the essence and quality of such – and stand firm in that sense of being. Be devoted to being.

Beyond A Mere Commitment

When we talk about devotion, we generally understand it to mean loyalty or enthusiasm about a person or cause. Many even are put in the mindset of worship. As stated before, I would like for you to think about this as more than just being committed to something. I want you to think about it in the sense of truly planting yourself and focusing your being toward another person and cause. More so the person than the cause. Being relationship ready will truly require that you rid yourself of the hindering fears associated with devoting yourself to another person.

We often talk about people being afraid of commitment. Sometimes, I wonder if the real fear is not commitment, but devotion. You see, commitment can be simply giving your word and following through with action. Devotion is more like giving yourself. This of course includes, attitudes, actions, and overall accountability. It requires the real you to show up. There isn't much room for masks here. As a matter of fact, your masks will complicate the matter. Authenticity is extremely important if devotion is to really be devotion. There is no doubt in my mind that devotion is one of the greatest manifestations of Love.

It's funny (not really), that many of the people I talk to about relationships always seem to be so burned, so scorned or so disappointed, that the idea of devotion to another person is avoided at all cost. This says a lot to me. Aside from the fact that obviously these people feel no one has ever been truly devoted to them, neither are they willing to tap into such a thing. It says to me that fear is often what is guiding us, despite the deep longing and desire to have a life filled with Love. Sometimes, I sense that the reason the trending #LoveYourself and #SelfLove is so popular is because it has been many people's only resort. Or at least it seems to them like it's their only resort.

In all fairness, I totally understand why. In many situations, we have truly let one another down. We have been exposed to some really bogus stuff. We have been disregarded. Likewise, we have dished out some of the same. When our experiences are filled with an abundance of disappointment and a seeming lack of being Loved well. The fear of devotion and all this jazz I am talking about is to be expected. You can't plant rutabagas (I think them things are NAS-and-TY), and expect to get Watermelons. Where they do that at? Yep, you guessed it ... right here on earth.

When we avoid or refrain from filling the world with what it needs to thrive, we are left to methods required to survive. Unfortunately, that is the mode many many people are in as it relates to life and relationships. We are seemingly in a mode of surviving one another. However, if we all were to approach our relationships with one another by casting fear away with Love and issuing pure devotion, we wouldn't have to survive one another. We would be putting in not just the work, but the wisdom that cause us all to thrive. But, as long as we are in fear and allowing it to rule; we will never truly know this thriving as we should. We will continue to think this relationship talk is just idealism or fairytale.

If we are going to be ready for relationships, we have to be willing and ready to choose beyond the presenting fear. Yes, it is true that we can get hurt and feel like we are wasting our time devoting to people who are only going to fail us or not return the same devotion. Truth, however, is that if we don't get beyond this fear, we are ultimately playing a game with one another and leading one another on. Or basically, dealing the energy of fear into the relationships that we claim to be ones for Love.

So much of our lives are filled with efforts to self-preserve, but what we often fail to realize is that if we collectively preserved, we might have tapped into one of the best ways to self-preserve without even needing additional effort. We can put our energy toward a cause much greater than our own self. One that will surprisingly support us by its own virtue once established as a whole. Particularly speaking about the relationship you are in or in preparation for, when you take this bigger picture devotion approach, you are fueling your relationship with thriving power that will support you and your partner. You are in essence taking the high road to relationships.

I said it once and will say it again – and a million times, the high road to true connection and oneness is found in devotion and being devoted to one another. Again, the true journey of Love is ultimately the discovery of oneness. Your ability to connect, be authentically present and give space for others to feel comfortable and secure in doing the same is invaluable. It is the greatest blessing we can give one another.

Worth-ship

Worth-ship! No, this is not a misspelling of the word worship. It is however a breakdown of the word. You see, generally speaking, when many people hear the word worship, they may imagine things like bowing down, waving hands, singing songs, crying out to God with promises they can't keep, or words of praise they themselves don't even understand. While this is definitely an application of the word – rightfully and traditionally directed toward a deity, I would like to invite you into an expanded use of this.

The word worship in its simplest – layman's terms, can be better understood as worth-ship. Now according to "the Google" (don't act like you don't know "the Google" knows everything you want it to know), the word basically comes from an Old English term weorþscipe, which means to regard with great respect, honor, and reverence. However, unless you have studied Old English, I am sure you are wondering how to pronounce that "w" word just mentioned. Well, sorry friend, keep wondering, I am not an English teacher nor linguist; you're on your own. Anyway, the word connotes worthiness or worth-ship. It means to give worth to something; or someone.

Now, before you say that worship belongs to no man but God, perhaps I should say that God is not a man. Considering this is not a book about theology, I won't go there (I just wanted to act petty cause it seemed fun). However, I do want to suggest as a mode of authenticity in your quest, refreshing or restoration in being relationship ready, that understanding what it really means to give worth to someone is valuable beyond words. While many may feel that it is inappropriate to use the word worship in regard to how we deal with one another, please for a moment, really dig deep into what we should see when we see another being made in the image and likeness of the Creator. We should see, the Creator's essence. Unfortunately, we often get stuck at only seeing people's personalities, vices and LeAnzar's good looks! Oh wait, I meant to say, their good looks. Anyway, as divine beings, spiritual beings, living souls, and balls of hot air and gas (ok scratch that last part), what we should see when we truly look at and see one another, is something or someone divine. We should see an emanation of God.

For some reason it seems, we are often afraid to see one another this way. I suppose the fear of being accused as an idol worshiper or someone who worships man, could play a huge part in why this idea may be hard for some people. In all reality, people are allowed to believe how they believe and appropriate this as they choose. However, the overall purpose of devotion I am speaking of in being relationship ready is not really to dive deep into the subscribed beliefs of people. Ultimately, what I want you to walk away with is the principle that is at work in the depths of true devotion, that derives from the spirit of our being. What I am talking about is not about being egotistical for oneself or majorly stroking the ego of another person. I am not suggesting or encouraging what many religious people might call fleshly worship. What I am really talking about is simply embodying the essence and fullness of what it may mean to Love someone and to be devoted to them. If you're really going to Love someone, you might as well give it all you've got. Please do not miss the overall principle of what I am getting at just because my expressions in stating it is not quite the way you would prefer it be stated.

As I was saying, we often have blockages to truly seeing one another divinely. I mentioned earlier that oftentimes we seem to be subtly relationship negative. It can seem like we live as enemies one to another. This alone makes it difficult to see one another as divine beings. There is a remnant of people that might actually admit to seeing others as divine, but for the vast majority of people, divine might not be the word choice.

Now, when I say see other as divine, I am not necessarily talking about some super deep, supernatural, angelic moment of seeing the person floating in the sky or needing to call them a god. I am simply speaking about recognizing that they too are spiritual beings manifest on this planet to have a human experience. It's that simple. It is a matter of knowledge and recognition. Granted, in order to fully process this, one might need to have an eye-opening experience of enlightenment or awakening – but even that doesn't have to be considered deep or mystical. Basically, what I am saying is don't make this harder than you need to. Sometimes the talk of spirituality, souls, etc., can get a bit complicated for people because we try to turn it into experiences beyond practical living. It can definitely include that, but please, for your own sake, don't box the spiritual experience into that.

Our boxes, and blockages are potentially the major hindrances to truly seeing one another. I get it. Some of the blockage is a result of us seeing how vile people can be. Heck, that would definitely hinder us from seeing them as divine and worthy of devotion.

Do you know the number one reason coupled relationships fail? Many think the biggest issues lie around cheating, communication issues, finances or sex. But reality is the main reason breakups happen is because of contempt. It is when we basically see ourselves as better than, greater than or more important that our relational partners. This contempt of course leads us to not knowing how to fight well, collaborating well and dealing with issues as a team and partners. Instead we deal as enemies and separate entities. Keeping the deep sense of worth at the forefront of our minds is important to overcoming contempt. Little things to keep a sense of admiration and adoration or even fondness for our significant others will help us tremendously in overcoming the vices we meet in them.

Sometimes, even something as pleasurable as our desires can be a hindrance to truly seeing one another. Let me explain.

It goes without saying that we live in a society that is currently obsessed and/or preoccupied with feeling good, being happy and "loving themselves." We pretty much go hard for this at almost any cost. Sometimes it is deliberate; other times, just compulsion and impulse taking over. Regardless of what is governing it, let's be straight, we all want to feel good, be happy and touch on ourselves. Ooops! Wait! Darn auto-correct made me say the wrong thing. I meant to say, we all want to feel good, be happy and love ourselves. You get the point. LOL.

Simply put, our desires have a way of taking over sometimes. They will often lead what we are willing to do or not do. They play a huge role in who we will engage for relationship, who we will have sex with, who we will bend over backwards for. I mean the list could go on and on. Other than work and a few things here and there, many of us may find ourselves hijacked by our desires – doing only what we want. This plays out in the heart of our devotion to others as well.

I am not saying that desires are bad – nor that giving into them are always bad. The problem comes in when we are so obsessed with pleasure and getting what we want, the way we want it, when we want it, etc., we increase the risk of missing people (even our partners) for who they really are as a divine being worthy of devotion, care, honor, respect and being treated with dignity.

If we move into a space where we only see them as fit for serving our own desires, we have discounted them and disregarded their divine relational worth. It's gloriously divine for a person to be the object of your devotion; but potentially belittling for them to be subject to your desire. I will say that again for the people in the back. If you are truly going to be in a healthy relationship, you have to work this out properly. Being relationship ready means, you recognize that to be the object of one's devotion is much more aligned than simply being subjected to one another's desires.

It is imperative to understand that being desired is not the same as being Loved; necessarily. While desiring and being desired can ignite some amazing feelings, it is Love ultimately that leads to filling and healing. When we live lives devoted to one another, we move beyond the consumer type of love and into the contributive and creative type of Love. The kind that speaks to another's worth beyond just our desire for them. We speak more aligned to our design to thrive with them.

I don't know about you, but when I am in my desire ... like really in it, I can be a beast. I have told many people that I am fully aware of the fact that I am a creature of desire. When I say creature ... I mean creatures. It's almost as if the creation of the divine has gone subject to the beast and creature of desire instead of creativity of design.

Think about it in terms of cooking versus eating. When you are cooking, you are actually building, sharpening skills, and even literally forming new connections in your brain that didn't exist or needed to be put to work. When you eat, on the other hand, you are not necessarily using your brain all that much. Love is like that. Are you creating with devoted passion and purpose, or are you just consumed or consuming in pleasure and pursuit?

I have stated many times that I try to refrain from sexual activity when I am "too" horny. When I am experiencing this, I don't even see the other person as a person, let alone aim to engage in a procreative process of enhancing the life of another being. It's almost like I see them just as a piece of meat to satisfy my cravings and lust. If you ever find me in a Brazilian Steak House, you'd see what I mean. I can devour some good meat. Sad huh? Yeh, well, in my heart of hearts, I have no desire to dishonor people like that. Even if they are in just as deep of a state, while it may be "hott" with two t's in the moment, later I feel horrible in my soul.

You see, my devotion to living from the higher me, is inclusive. It's not just about me. The higher me recognized the value, worth, importance and interdependence of others. No, I have not mastered any of this. I am only able to carry this out on a good day. Catch me on a bad day and you'd be questioning who in the hell wrote this book. That being said, don't catch me Mondays, Tuesdays, Wednesdays, Thursday mornings, Fridays, Saturdays after 6am, or Sunday between 9am and midnight. You might run into a beast of a different kind.

No. Truth is, I do truly practice what I preach. I just haven't mastered it. Ultimately folks, we have to understand that when we are full on in our devotion, we learn to ascribe worth to one another. Devotion becomes about that; nothing less.

As one who sharpens his or her sense of devotion, you become a "worth-shiper" (you like what I did there with that word? Thanks, God gave it to me right on the spot). It ends up not being something that you have. It ends up becoming or being something that you really are. In essence, you become the ship that carries worth in its loins – distributing it as a reminder to every soul you encounter so that they are seen, known and Loved. If this is not something that

45

you are ready to ascribe to a relationship, you might do better to refrain from subjecting someone to something otherwise engaged.

Embodying what it means to be a worth-shiper, not only are you aware of who you are and the divine relational worth you're endowed with, but you help others see, remember and experience it within themselves. If you are in a relationship with someone, this should be a mutual and reciprocal relational consciousness dealt from one to another. Or at least, that is a wise way to go about it. It is in these spaces that we thrive. Does it always pan out that the reciprocity is a perfect match? Maybe not. But again, in these spaces we are better suited to thrive.

You have to get rid of the idea that you are losing yourself. Again, devotion is not about losing out or giving your rights away. It's about standing in righteousness and giving the fullness of your Love. Giving yourself as Love. It's not giving up on yourself; it's giving of yourself. You can only do that when you are being yourself. If you aren't being yourself, not only are you cheating your relational partner; but you are cheating yourself as well. You are depriving your relationship of the soundness, security and spirit it needs to thrive.

As a worth-shiper – or worth shipper, you are literally carrying fruit that will nourish your relationship in every season. You carry and produce worth when you deal patiently with your partner. When you are a space of peace and joy, you are reminding your partner of their worth. You see that goodness you carry, pulls on their divineness. When you deal in gentleness you are letting them know they are worth such grace. Now, I know some of y'all like it rough, but we ain't talking about that right now. Get yo' mind right. LOL. Anyway, when you honor your partner with faithfulness and even embrace the virtue of self-control, you my friend, are saying to your partner, "I am devoted ... and you are worth it."

Truth be told, you are also saying it to yourself. There is such a deep oneness to all of this, that perhaps some of the commentary for self and self that is not really all that necessary.

CHAPTER Y

YIELD FACTOR

You know, sometimes it seems like most of the pre-relationship advice out there is center around watching for red flags. While there can be a time and season for anything, the red flag approach to relationships can really play into our relationship negative energy if we aren't careful. That negative mentality will potentially lead us not only to self-righteousness, but also toward further singleness. This may even be one of the primary reasons we often hear people (not you, I am talking about other people) say, "I can't find anyone." Is it possible that you... I mean, they are focusing on red flags, instead of recognizing the sign on the road that says, "YIELD?"

Times have driven us into a place of truly having to fend for ourselves. While there is a need for everyone to bear their own cross in life; there is also the real need that we should also bear one another's burdens when the call is before us. Having to fend for ourselves, has in some ways landed us with ill or mixed feelings about one another. Our lives have become about self-preservation so much so that often even when we think of engaging relationships, we are obsessed with figuring out how it serves us.

Sometimes, this leads to a tainting of our service to others because it turns out that our service is based on their service.

Yes, relationships should be reciprocal in some way. However, when we are overburdened by having to fend for ourselves – which often is laced in surviving others, we are essentially living in defense for ourselves. It's very hard to navigate a relationship in a healthy manner when our defenses are up or when we feel like we are left to take care of ourselves. A truth often ignored, avoided or aborted in relationships is interdependence. Stuck in a mode of fending for and defending the self, can truly lead us to forget that we are in this together. It will inevitably divide our team. Living in a defense and red flag mode leads us to stop signs instead of a gracious flow with yield signs.

What's all this talk about yield signs Zar? Well, I am glad you asked. If we are to be at all ready for relationships, we have to embrace the virtue of yielding. When we are moving full steam ahead in our relationship goals, but void of a good sense of yielding to another person's experience, needs and wants, we are essentially living a relationship negative life. Being ready for the relationship you want without being mindful of the relationship your partner wants or needs, will potentially make you selfish. Not to mention, leave the two of you in contempt at some point and potentially resentful and bitter.

Yes, you can say, "well maybe we just aren't compatible." The question however is, how true is that? There are many people, even "soul mates," that to this day are not engaged in relationship with one another because the thought was that they are incompatible, got on one another's nerves, or did something that was a reflection of human frailty or faultiness. Many couples have ended their relationship with someone that was actually fit for them, thinking that they weren't because of a disillusionment phase or stage in the relationship. Many friends never progressed to be a couple because of missed marks of some sort. Ultimately, many relationships never happen or end because the art and heart of yielding was missing. It wasn't incompatibility. Maybe it was relational incompetence, lack of self-awareness, self-control, an abundance of self-righteousness, a lack of yielding ... or perhaps it was underdeveloped character.

While there may be times when we are supposedly incompatible, and some people who are pursuing romantic relationship together shouldn't, it is very questionable that we are all this darn incompatible. The divorce rates are ridiculous. The amount of cutting each other off simply results in a bloody massacre. It's one that many people are priding themselves on, all in the name of protecting their energy and "deserving" better.

Again, I am not saying that everyone should be together in the coupling sense. However, every failed relationship or encounter with another person that somehow rubs you the wrong way, is not necessarily a case of incompatibility. Many times, our relationships end simply because of pride, fear, hardness of the heart or a lack of submission. There are many relationships that fail because of power struggles in surviving one another's role expectations instead of thriving in "whole expectations." Operating in roles versus wholeness can cause major problems because this forces people into trying to fulfill their partner's dream, instead of living out their own awakening. When we set intentional vision & focus in partnering in wholeness, any roles and positions that may be necessary can birth from that abundance. So, many times relationships end simply because we weren't ready to put into it the thrive juice that it required of us. I mean, God forbid something is required of us ... who wants that; Geesh! We want the acquire – not require. Right?

Well, if that is you, then ... you might have to look at what kind of spirit and energy you are mastering. How much of your core essence in being Love, is being masked?

Make Way

You may find that there are a couple of definitions for yielding. One definition means to give way. The other means to provide and produce what's needed to thrive. Both of these definitions are warranted wisdoms to be welcomed warmly by relationship ready weirdos. Ok, I got a little carried away with the w's, but you get the point.

If we really want to talk about making Love. We have to understand yielding. Making Love means making way for one another. It simply is a new perception of submission.

In any relationship, there can be a colliding instead of collaboration. There may be some huge traces of power struggles and systems of hierarchy lurking in the relationship. The talk of dominance versus submission can be included here. A common structure set up in heterosexual relationships seems to be the talk about the man being the leader or head and the women submitting to that leadership or headship. In many homosexual relationships, there is the talk about tops or bottoms, generally where the top is viewed as the dominant one and the bottom as the submissive one. Then there are those relationships where a wife may seem overbearing and the husband considered to be weak. On occasion there comes the couple where both are a bit too much for anyone to handle because they are both aggressive; and that mouth just leads to the rise of "these hands." I mean, in all reality, these are just examples of how the systems of hierarchy, power struggles, possible collisions, etc., can play out. I am sure you can come up with some of your own. I just used these because they are common.

The bottom line is, we often approach the idea of relationships with the idea that someone is the leader and the other is the follower. One person is dominant and the other is submissive. One person is the provider and the other person is the recipient. These ideas, believe it or not, have an ability to perpetuate a social construct and misappropriation of power within us all.

Although there exists within humanity and the universe, masculine and feminine energy (and people), it is only fair to further realize that this energy is actually present in all of us. Additionally, the energy would be more about balance than it would be about dominating or hierarchy. The characteristics typically associated with femininity are not to be considered as weakness under masculinity. Nor should the characteristics typically associated with masculinity be considered as strengths over femininity. In all reality, they are both positive qualities – and strengths if you will, particularly when they are in operation and obedience to one another as they should be.

For the record, the "should be" is not determined by force. It should be determined by flow, grace and what's needed for us all to thrive in the moment and in life. And the word obedience, isn't about dictating to one another, it's about dedicating movement and action toward another. It's about living together in a choreographed flow that promotes and enhances our ability to thrive and build one another up in Love.

You see, ultimately, it's about balance and making way for one another. When this is in operation, we are not at odds, we are compliments. We are in Love. We are both submitting to one another and leading. Making way for one another or yielding in this sense, makes us a team.

You must embrace what it means to be yielding. This is a sure word of wisdom for you in your stance as a relationship ready person. Again, it requires courage just like devotion does. It's not merely courage to take a chance, it's courage to be the change ... the change the world and our way of dealing with one another needs. You will be tempted to fight for your way to a self-win; but please don't be so sold on that that you lose the one you say you Love.

Don't be so consumed with your, "I don't," that you never end up being ready to say, "I do."

I am not telling you not to have a standard. I am saying be the standard. I am not telling you to be a doormat. I am however telling you it's wise to be ready and willing to wash the feet of your Loved one. I am not telling you to not consider yourself or any of the other things people like to throw in as rebuttals to yielding to your partner. What I am saying is that you can't be so stuck in your ways, (or on your ways) that you subject your partner to having to fend for him or herself. Make way for them. And be present while you do it. I will say this again. Make way for them and be fully present while you do it.

If it becomes a problem that your needs are not being met, then please, have the conversation. As a matter of fact, doing so, gives them the opportunity to exercise their creative power in Love toward you. However, don't allow yourself to fall subpar to giving the relationship the higher you, simply because the knucklehead is being complacent or absentminded. At the end of the day, all you can do is your part to be built up in Love.

Provide and Honor

I am sure you've heard it stated, "divide and conquer." Well this ain't that. You are preparing to be a contributing player on a team. You aren't looking to divide your partner into pieces or conquer and lord over them. You are in this to be the best relational partner you can be. As you embrace the definitions of what it means to be yielding, don't forget the part about providing and producing what is needed to thrive.

Yes, you are making way for your partner, but you also have to provide and produce something that sets them and your relationship on a course for thriving. When we embrace this, we are simply exercising the wisdom and good sense that God gave us. The deep inner part of your soul is no stranger to this wisdom. Actually, it is the very reason your soul seeks out another. It is the reason souls recognize loneliness. It is the reason it knows pain and has some degree of desire for expression. The soul knows something our life experiences sometimes doesn't always afford the opportunity to hold on to for long. The soul knows a song the lips have never sung. It knows thriving. Even if experiencing it fully hasn't manifested. The soul knows thriving, because it was created in it. Believe it or not, surviving is sort of a foreigner for the spirit-soul.

Oftentimes, the dark night of the soul, is just that, a dark night, because the soul is ultimately no stranger to its Light Source. It knows it's home. You see, this is why we are often upset at injustice. It's foreign to the soul. This is why we cry when someone hurts us. It is not because we don't have our big boy drawers on, or big girl panties on (or big boy panties and big girl drawers ... whatever you wear). It's because the soul knows it was worth something more than the degrading it had just received. The reason pain indicates something is wrong, is because it's trying to alert us of something foreign going on ... something potentially infectious if not tended to immediately and properly.

Embodying the virtue of yielding in a relationship in terms of providing and producing, is crucial in that is brings nourishment to the table. You are in essence providing a substance that can feed your relationship and keep it strong throughout every season. This provision can and should manifest in multiple ways.

Usually when we talk about providing, people automatically go to financial or material things. Yes, this can be a manifestation; however, it is not the only manifestation. Arguably, it may not even be the primary manifestation. What if the primary manifestation of provision is the ascribing of worth? What if it was somehow the manifestation of the divine within our being, being allowed to surface as itself in all of its Christ-ness? What if one of the greatest provisions of a relationship was simply being able to freely be who or what we were designed to be?

I am not saying that we shouldn't eat and all that. Please, this is an area where I am really calling for you to unlock your spiritual intelligence and for you to emanate from the Divine. What if the greatest provision we could offer to one another, was the space to be, grow, align, shine, etc.? I can imagine from that place, we still could have the various material possessions manifest. Just ponder that for a while. Perhaps, this is what unconditional Love is really about. Maybe the unconditional is the providing of conditions that will allow us to be who we are without the threat of being subjected to a lesser sense of worth as a member of the whole.

We provide for our relationships when we see the divine in one another and respond accordingly. Namaste. I know some of this may sound a bit farfetched and maybe even impractical to some of you all, but really, it's not. It's actually very practical and can manifest in practical ways. It all simply boils down to the wisdom of having productive relationships. Productive, doesn't necessarily mean we have indulged the social constructs have created great businesses or children together. Productive can simply mean, we have birthed the kind of Love that is reflective of God. It can mean we have built homes of acceptance for one another. It can mean that we see to it that our team goes undivided. It can mean that our procreative power has been used not just to make more humans, but to make the human experience more meaningful and fuller in the production of the fruit of the Spirit.

Not every relationship will have children, but every relationship should procreate and have fruit. There can be a spiritual achievement that harnesses any physical or natural accomplishment.

Responsibility and Response Ability

Yielding is not just our responsibility in a relationship. It is also and more fittingly our ability to respond in a relationship. Now this can be viewed a few ways as well. We often hear people talk about reacting versus responding. In this use of such phrasing, we find that reacting is usually an automatic reflex to some stimuli, good or bad. Responding, is usually more intentional and thought through.

If we are to embrace the idea of oneness in our preparation for relationships, we have to understand that comes with responsibility. Even though people always say, we are not responsible for anyone else, this is sort of a misconception. There are some things to be considered here. The truth is, we affect one another. For this reason alone, we have to at least embrace some level of responsibility TO one another. In some ways, this goes back to our talk about accountability. We have to do our work. Doing our work, leads to the work of the collective, even if the collective doesn't embrace the charge.

You can argue this, but you will lose. No, I am kidding, you might win, however, I would like to invite you into a perspective on this. I personally sense that it is our responsibility to walk according to the spirit of our being. Tying all this together – simply because it is the greatest manifestation of ourselves and therefore the greatest contribution we can provide to our relationships. It is the best we can do at reflecting the Image and likeness in which we were made. It is how we do our part to be built up in and as Love.

As we do these things and take on the charge of being the most authentic to our essence, we strengthen our response ability, or ability to respond, instead of just reacting when faced with whatever we will be faced with. The virtue of yielding positions us to respond to the various relationship challenges we will face. It positions us with an upper hand to respond to temptations, instead of just reacting to them (oftentimes the reaction of giving into them). When faced with the urge to quit, yielding positions us to respond in faithfulness. Yielding, positions us to respond with patience instead of punching when our relational partner gets on our first and last nerve. The yielding virtue positions us to respond with honoring a desire or wish of our partner when we would have otherwise reacted selfishly. You see, this can be really powerful in bringing or producing Love in our relationships, instead of fear and a need to survive one another or to force our way.

Our ability to respond becomes a key component to what's grown and harvested in our relationships. Yielding simply helps us lift one another. I know you might see it as lowering yourself, but when you really understand the heart of this, you can know that ultimately you rose to the occasion. The occasion of oneness, honor, caring and Love. Even when it makes you cringe a little. Many times, we are cringing over things that don't really matter in the long run anyway.

In the book, *The Secret Life of Bees* (Sue Monk Kidd, November 2001), the story is told of how May wanted to paint the house this bold pink color. While the color was considered odd and outright hideous for a house, the older sister, August, saw that that color really brightened May's day. May already struggled with deep feelings of sadness over many of the perils of life and sensing the hurt of others. August Loved her sister and really spoke to her worth by agreeing to paint the house the color May wanted. August decided that instead of reacting to the horrid color, she would graciously respond by choosing what really mattered. Her sister's joy. She realized that the color of a house isn't what really matters in life, but the joy in that house along with the people in it meant way more. She stated, "Lifting someone's heart, now that matters." She yielded. Not just in making way for her sister to have what she wanted, but also in providing and producing a space where her sisters was honored and cared for. She created grounds for joy to flow. That is what mattered.

If we are to be relationship ready, we have to understand what really matters. If it is not the life and heart of others, we might be trying to pursue the wrong kind of relationship or just pursuing it out of selfishness. We have to be willing to look at what really matters. When faced with differences, are you willing to take the mature road of responding to choose what really matters? Does the color of the house really matter – so much so that you potentially lose the relationship? Or does the person matter more?

Of course, the house reference is just a metaphor to represent so many other relational differences or challenges we may face. Sex, recreation, sex as recreation, finances, goals, dreams, pet peeves, heck, pets ... can all be things that pop up in our relationships as smoke screens or issues that can potentially divide our team.

Yielding virtue, brings us to the responsibility and response ability of being considerate of our partner. Take sex for example. Ask yourself this question. Are you or are you willing to be sexually considerate of your partner? Now, only you know what the heck y'all do or want to do in the bedroom, so I won't go into specifics. However, is that experience going to be about just your pleasure, or will you consider your partner? Will you be so consumed with climax that your miss the opportunity for connection? Is it all about them making your toes tingle but you rush them through their process? Is it just about what you will and won't do or are you willing to consider some things that may not necessarily be your forte, but because they matter you can learn to enjoy that they enjoy some things.

Oftentimes, we make the mistake of trying to enjoy the exact same thing and if we don't, we scream incompatibility and no chemistry. Sometimes, we have to reassign purpose for some of our engagements. For example, every act of sex might not be for personal pleasure. Perhaps it could be primarily for connection. I suggest that couples not just have sex when they are horny and trying to just get off. It might be wise and important to include some sexual experiences (could be intercourse or not), that aren't necessarily for the physical pleasure, but ultimately the soul's pleasure which is connection, care and tending to. If we only engage because of pleasure, we are setting ourselves up for failure in being well versed relationally and a lacking in strength to have a relationship based on much more.

Presence should be one of the most powerful things in a relationship because it is a double portion of the Divine in the mix. From that presence and connection can birth so many wonderful things ... including pleasures, but not limited to them. However, we must be intentional. Not saying we need to be routine or so planned in a way that takes away the mystery, spontaneity, spice or romance. I am saying we must do the work of yielding to what matters. I sense that from there, if done in purity, we can still have a deeply spicy relationship. But part of yielding is willingness.

Sexual consideration takes willingness. And again, it also takes the wisdom to assign multiple purposes for your sexual experiences together. Some experiences will be to make a baby, some will be for just satisfying pleasures, some will be for connection, some for the video camera (I don't know who that was for)! Anyway, I'm really saying, don't just have one purpose for your engagements and be sure to take time to be considerate of your partner. Yield.

The same goes for other aspects of the relationship. Because my love language is primarily quality time, I tend to not be overly concerned with the activities of my relationship. Regarding my really close friends, I remember saying that we could have a great time doing nothing. This is because my relationship with them wasn't about the activities. It was about my adoration of them and admiration for them. It might be wise to adopt a heart that is concerned with adoration and admiration instead of activity. Winnie the Pooh said it best, "doing nothing leads to the very best of something." There can be so much Love, joy and fun in just being in the same vicinity of your partner. I mean there can also be so much boredom and frustration too ... but we are trying to be relationship positive here so take that thought captive until we are done with this book. LOL.

No, really, doing things in relationships are cool and an inevitable must. However, as we mature in our relational wisdom, we have to stay abreast of the power and purpose of relationships. We have to stay mindful of the persons in the relationship and allow the activities to be additives, not the definitive of the relationship. But when we truly set out to Love the person we are in relationship with, we are strengthening the bond and allowing the very best of something to happen as it may.

Now, I only used a couple examples here for the yielding thing, but it applies to any area of relationship that may arise. Being considerate has to play out in all aspects. Afterall, the relationship is just that – a relationship. It's not just you in it. There are others to be considered and hopefully they are considering you. When both parties of a relationship are truly being considerate of one another, neither has to force their hand or force their way or fend for themselves. As a matter of fact, when done properly, we can relax because ultimately, we know the other person has us and will do whatever they can to help us thrive. We can set our focus on Loving them and allow them to set their focus on Loving us. You can still keep your self-love, but you might find that it is rare that you would ever even have to use those terms as some kind of cut out time. At some point, it all should begin to follow seamlessly but truth is, Love is not divided from self and other ... it is all ONE. The challenge is finding yourself healthy enough in it to recognize it and being with others who have had the same revelation.

Produce Good

As you set yourself toward unlocking your spiritual intelligence and relational wisdom of yielding, there are points to ponder and remember. Yielding isn't about lowering yourself; it is about rising to the occasion of Love. It is about considering and honoring another. Of course, this message is to everyone, so that means that you should be having this virtue bestowed upon you as well; but we can't control what others will do. You have to be solid and undivided enough within yourself to manifest this virtue because you know it is wisdom; not just because others are going to give it back to you.

Remember, yielding is a matter of making way and providing that which is necessary for thriving. In order to truly produce the right spirit of your relationship, it can't be about you making the person a means to an end for your own pleasure, climaxes, stimulation or love for certain activities. When we do this, we reduce them to a function instead of a fellow. That's just not kind. That is sowing selfishness into your relationship. You can't sow selfishness into your relationship and expect a harvest of true Love. That would be like sowing watermelon seeds in the ground but expecting tomatoes to grow. Where they do that at? Stop it.

The reality of all this is, you have to be bold enough to put into your relationship the pure spirit and energy that produces good. I have seen countless relationships (like the ones we discussed at the start of this book) that look good, but when you search the intentions, purity and inner workings, they simply aren't producing good. The yielding is off. The manipulation is high; and even the chemistry works a lot of times for some parts, but the energy ultimately is ... for lack of better words – draining! The couple is left surviving one another instead of thriving with and from one another.

CHAPTER 6

ENLIGHTENED RELATIONSHIPS

With just a little bit of recap, relational readiness is really not a matter of just being eager for one. While that is nice, it will not be what is necessary for creating and maintaining a successful partnership. Being relationship ready is neither just a matter of having something in our human design that draws us toward them. Because we live in a time and age where there are so many different perspectives, philosophies, cultural upbringing and environmental shaping, the varying differences have led to what seems like a cause to have to survive one another; instead of thrive – with and from one another.

We have unfortunately been placed in positions that lead us more toward defending ourselves than extending ourselves. We are oftentimes drawn more toward complaining that we deserve better treatment, instead of simply aligning to our worth. We are subjecting ourselves to fear-based, relationship negative energies instead of the wisdom of relational consciousness that aims toward soul level win wins for us all. It goes without saying that we are in need of enlightened relationships. I think we have always needed them, however I think it's now more than ever, a great time to align or realign ourselves to what it really means to be in relationship to and with one another (I am sure that every generation of humans have made this statement though).

While, what I am saying is a general statement to any type of relationship, significant other relationships that are highly influenced by romantic desire, etc. are no exception to this high time for alignment. It is often the romantic partnerships that lead to family, which leads to community and a foundational place for how society members are shaped. Basically, what I am saying is that partnerships are important because they lead to something much greater than themselves, even if they don't specifically come to a place of raising children. As we have seen in today's social media outlets, relationships are highlighted and trending. In other words, people follow them and seek to be like many of the couples they see. When people see something good or presumably good, they can't help but want the same things and inquire about how to get, create or develop it. This is not a bad thing. Unless, the relationships being modeled are fronts, frauds and fakes. While being in relationships with your #Boo, #Bae, or #Beau is pretty personal, it still has the potential and perhaps even the responsibility to reflect a bigger picture; influencing or guiding others toward what it really means to Love.

Aside from the societal effect of relationships, there is the effect they have on your own soul. Operating from principles of an enlightened relationship is quite frankly, just wisdom. It is the enlightened relationships that lead our souls toward thriving. Enlightenment for relationships lead us to somewhat of a safeguarding for our souls. This doesn't mean we won't still get hurt or have some mishaps. It simply means we are aligning it to the positive energy and holy spirit it was designed for ... and in. When this alignment is central, not only are you positioned to contribute to a healthy and whole relationship, but you are also positioned to receive from them. You see, it ends up being a reciprocal process that leaves neither partner gasping for air. You are able to pour and be poured into. You can navigate in a way that doesn't subject one another to the need to survive one another's constant foolishness. Instead, you are able to _____ (fill in the blank, because I have said it so much now that you should know it by heart). Ok, the answer is "thrive."

I am sure you have noticed that this thrive word seems to be a running theme in this whole relationship ready talk. This is because ultimately, enlightened relationships are all about thriving. Thriving as a couple, a team and even thriving as a community. I couldn't think of a "c" word for individual self, but enlightened relationships are about thriving individually too. Ironically enough, it is all connected. So many people try to separate it, but reality is, that is often a fear-based approach to living life. Again, fear-based approaches are in essence negative energy at work; yet they are expected to create positive outcomes. If we could really see how this doesn't truly help the team, I think we'd shift our dealings.

It is so important to realize just what an enlightened relationship is. For the most part, it is one where both partners are in the relationship with one another, working toward and/or exuding their higher selves. Yes, enlightened relationships are about more than just having someone to lay next to at night. It is more than just having a partner to satisfy your insatiable desires or to stroke your ego. It's all about us aligning to our divine selves and continuing the life-giving breath of God in one another. Moreover, (I always wanted to use that word) it is about having someone walk alongside you in experiencing, navigating, creating and contributing to life.

While typical romantically based relationships have gotten us through the ego needs at times. It is enlightened relationships that will get us to soul satisfaction – and beyond that, soul fulfillment. When I say soul fulfillment, I am not talking about gratification, I am more so talking about fulfilling the purpose our soul exists and has manifested on this planet.

Considering all this, let's look at the difference between typical relationships and enlightened relationships. Instead of reinventing the wheel, I want to share with you just a few of the things we teach in relationship workshops using the Enlightened Relationships Workbook (Transformation Publishing).

Typical Relationship: *Characteristics:*	**Enlightened Relationship:** *Characteristics:*
Shared living environment	Shared interest and time
Shared responsibility	together
Friendship	Mutual support for growth
Physical intimacy	Emotional intimacy
	True companionship
Improve relationship with:	*Improve relationship with:*
Communication strategies	Creating a shared life vision
Compromise	Increasing quality time together
Remembering commonalities	Helping each other reach their
Accepting differences	potential
Becoming aware of triggers and	Improving the depth of your
patterns	connection
	Learn each other's love
NEED: Dependency/Enmeshment	language
Roles/Conflict	***WANT:*** Union
Growth Through Experience	Wholeness/Cooperation
	Conscious Growth

These characteristics hopefully serve as a clearer picture for helping you sort through and write the vision for the type of relationship that your soul can appreciate and find great joy in. We all know that the psychology of the human brain, mixed with already pre-conditioned thinking, definitions, etc., can lead to some extra confusion or dissonance. Therefore, it might be worth making a few comments of clarification or adding some fine print clauses ... that way, at least it might make you feel better about spending your coin on this book (smile).

The Meaning Making Clause

First let's point out that the highlighted differences of an enlightened relationship do not mean that there won't be some level of overlap to typical relationships. While enlightened relationships highlight shared interests and time together, it generally still embraces a shared living environment. Enlightened relationships are not void of shared responsibility, friendship or physical intimacy either. Enlightened relationships simply go deeper into what it means to be partners with a clearer picture of what our soul needs in order to thrive.

Talk to any relationship therapist, coach, or unsolicited advisor (smile), and you will definitely hear that communication is key to having a successful or improved relationship. While this is not wrong, we must understand that it must be qualified to an enlightened degree. We often communicate, even when we aren't communicating. Ha, figure that one out! Be aware that that the root word of communication is commune. This is all about connection, mutual sharing, etc. That being said, it's one thing to communicate something and another to make meaning together during that communication. It is extremely important. So instead of just saying that people need to have good communication skills, I tend to guide more toward making meaning together so that people are actually on the same page and at least relating to one another in regard to the same thing. How often have you heard someone say, "but I told them that xyz was a concern for me?" Following this is often, "but I didn't know that was what you meant." You see, we are communicating, but not really making meaning together; therefore, relationships suffer not from a lack of communication, but instead a plethora of either poor communication and a lack in making meaning together. When someone says they love you, you might want to ask what that means to and for them. This could save you a lot of time, trouble and tissue!

The Collaboration Clause

Another common phrase we hear is that relationships are about compromise. I am gritting my teeth even as I contemplate this idea. Again, this is not to say that this is wrong for people to say; however, maybe the goal should be collaboration and developing a shared life vision. Sure, there may be some back and forth regarding this, however in enlightened relationships, that back and forth is not necessarily a fight, but instead working our way through many of the things that seek to divide our team.

The whole idea of compromise in relationship is inevitable to a huge degree, however it shouldn't be the heart of our life together necessarily. I only say this because the mentality often taken with the idea of compromise is that someone has to give up something; in turn lose out on something. We go in not only knowing that we will have to compromise, but this is something we expect our partners to do as well. This can sometimes play negatively on our brain and if we aren't careful, it can cause us to enter into the relationship from the start with a bit of silent resentment; especially if our partner of choice doesn't seem to be compromising as much as we do. Again (I say again a lot because some of this is hard to process and can be easily taken wrong), it's ok that our ego will have to let go of some of its reigns. What's more important is to remember and focus on the reality that relationships are a wise collaboration of the spirit more than it is a compromise of the ego.

Our dating phase is marked with statements that we are getting to know a person. The silent unspoken many times is we are really trying to find out if we are willing to compromise or how long we will be able to put up with the other person. Shhhhh, don't tell yourself that I told you that secret.

Friends, all I am saying is, is that in enlightened relationships, our engagement with a potential partner (or current partner)

68

should not just be to spend time with them to see if we can deal with them without them getting on our nerves too much. From an enlightened standpoint, you learn your partner to see how and if you can support them, care for them and compliment them.

Ok ... moving on before one of you all shoot me through this book!

The Trigger & Peace Clause

Speaking of shooting, let's look at the whole trigger aspect of things. The way this thing is set up, any and everything in our lives, at any moment, can be a trigger that bring up old wounds, past traumas, ill patterns of thinking, and unwise behaviors. I think this is something that we have to know will happen in relationship with another human being. Geesh, it might even happen while you are locked in your closet loving yourself with, "me time." To think that a close relationship will only rub you the "right way," is a bit of a setup, fantasy and romanticized perception of relationships. Did you know that even what we call "soul mate" relationships will potentially trigger unresolved or troubling issues within us? As a matter of fact, part of being in relationship of such nature, is a matter of helping one another reach our fullest potential, which also means helping one another heal. In order for this healing to happen, sometimes the wounds and trauma will be exposed to some degree.

Now of course I am not saying that our partners should purposely pick at our wounds, be abusive or misuse them in this regard; however, I am saying that if you are truly showing up in the relationship intimately, there will be some intimate things stepped on at times. When you dance closely, you might just happen to step on that corn on the left baby toe!

Being relationship ready means, you are both creating spaces where vulnerability is welcomed; with that comes the potential that you will be triggered in a great way. Many times, we aim to protect ourselves from ever being triggered. This is not necessarily a commitment to healing; this is a commitment to convenience. We in essence say, "I love you so long as you don't cause any of my trauma to resurface." Question is, is that how we heal? Or is that just how we cover up? Intimate relationships are about exposure, not closure. They are about being able to be as we are, but at the same time, being able to heal together when and where it is needed.

Oftentimes failed relationships are not the result of two people not being meant for one another. The failed relationship is sometimes the result of our unresolved grief, traumas or abuse, meeting the unresolved grief, traumas or abuse of the other person. We basically are then guided by our trauma, not our authentic selves. So then, the darkness of those elements are met with the darkness of our significant others, family or friends, thereby leading us into gross darkness covering the relational dealings instead of our light and our Love.

You see, ladies and gentlemen, just like the body was designed to be able to fight off sickness and even heal itself, our relationships rightly aligned can carry much of the same properties. If communion or relationship is at the core heart of our nature, then it would make sense that relationships are not only essential to our soul health, but also effective in healing it when necessary.

Considering this, maybe we should look deeper into some of the statements we adopt as full on truth. We often say that it is impossible for people to be in a relationship until they are healed. While this may carry some elements of truth to it, perhaps there is more. Perhaps, being in properly aligned relationship is what will actually help to heal them. Perhaps more than being fully healed in order to be in a successful relationship, what we really need a willingness to be healed in and by our relationships. Selah ... or sigh!

You might say, "well, keeping off the corns on my feet gives me the peace I need to be well in my relationships." Hmm ... No! Keeping off the corns on your feet gives you the undisturbed quiet you need; peace is something else.

The Hebrew word for peace is "shalom." It translates as, nothing missing, and nothing broken; also means intact, complete and in good health. You aren't healed nor at peace just because you've been in silence or sedation, and untriggered. Peace and healing come from gaining the proper alignment of wisdom and authenticity of our being in regard to the traumas that have harmed the harmonic flow of our lives and essential mode of relating. Peace and healing, is the realignment of our light in a dark world, ill experiences, etc.

I think maybe I should leave that piece of the conversation right there and allow you to process all of this before bullets start flying again. Just know, my heart is for your heart to truly heal and understand that within reason, there will be some rise or triggering of trauma if you are in a close relationship. It's important to remember that many times, your partner didn't cause the trauma, they potentially only triggered it. Don't make them responsible for matters you have suffered before them. Instead, ask them to join their most authentic being, with your most authentic being to help you heal. Afterall, wouldn't that be a part of partnering? Or did you just want them for the feels?

The W.O.W.

Enlightened relationships are marked with opportunities to learn yourself (and your partner) not just learning relationship skills and strategies ... some that are low key questionable as manipulation techniques. You see, relationships skills should be used as wisdom, not as ways to outwit your partner.

The more you embrace the wisdom of relationships, learn yourself and your partner, the better equipped you are to function effectively, and even affectionately in the relationship. Enlightened relationships grow more through you aligning consciously versus just depending on experiences. It is wiser to operate based on your alignment in the wholeness of who you are, versus on expected roles you are demanded to fill. I spoke earlier about the roles and how hierarchy can creep in there. That positions us to Lord over one another – which fuel power struggles. That can be a problem in enlightened relationships.

Now, I am not completely off my rocker. I understand that relationships are often very different for people as they are frequently viewed as more relative than absolute. My hopes here is not to present you with a box that your relationship must fit in, but instead I am just trying to present you with the W.O.W. or some Words Of Wisdom for how to manifest yourself in the great, yet sometimes frustrating, gift of relationships and oneness.

CHAPTER 7

LANDING THE RELATIONSHIP

I am sure you noticed that in the previous chapter, I said, "words of wisdom for how to manifest yourself." Not necessarily how to manifest a partner. Seems I can't get anything past your keen eyes (smile).

Often, we approach the idea of finding the right person to be in relationship with from the standpoint of landing the right one. While this is definitely not a discouragement from being in union and communion with someone that truly compliments you, I have to offer a word of wisdom here that may be helpful as you navigate this space. There is a lot of talk out there about how dating sucks and how difficult it is to find the right person. There is not as much talk embraced as to being the right person (it is stated, just not embraced as well). We tend to speak more about what we want from a relationship instead of who and what we want to be in a relationship.

Wait, my bad, we do sometimes talk about what we want to be in the relationship. Catered to ... comfortable and maybe spanked a little during naughty time. Inclusively, there is nothing wrong with that, however; we mustn't lose sight of our light.

Basically, instead of just seeking to land the right relationship, it might be helpful to position and present yourself in right standing with the relationship ready virtues mentioned in this book. When you do this, you then manifest as the land that a relationship can healthily thrive upon. Without such alignment, more energy will be exerted by your lover toward surviving. That is counterproductive to – "all that goodness" within you both. Our energy should be put toward being who and what we are; not toward who and what we are defending ourselves from.

When we are the land that is fertile for a relationship to grow, we are not just a cute place to fall in love. We become the land in which we can be built up in Love. As a matter of fact, we are the Love that is able to keep us from falling and present us faultless before the presence of God's glory with exceeding joy. That's bible right there! LOL.

Seriously though, we embrace and embody our divine relational worth in this regard. We truly are able to say to anyone coming into our garden space, "I am Love for you." Yes, #iAmLove4u. You see, this hashtag positions you to connect and increase engagement. You therefore increase the awareness within your relationship (potentially outside of it as well). Increased awareness leads to greater awakening and alignment of who we really are. Then, together, we can be greater support to one another in being the best version of ourselves. Now, if this alignment causes you to be on the radar as a person (and partnership) that is a true picture of what a healthy and Loving relationship looks like, GREAT; that is a relationship worth reacting to with #relationshipgoals. Additionally, when this happens, you in a way help to set divine order or influence to the way others seek to Love and relate. Not that it is your intention, but your standing in Love becomes a beacon of light in a dark and confusing world.

I know that I have said this time and time again, but I believe the repetition is worth it. Your healthy alignment is worth it. You have to understand that cultivation of the land can happen through relationship, so it's not about expecting everything to be perfect (without flaw or error), it's about being perfect (mature) and willing.

As stated before, being relationship ready is not a matter of being "over" past hurts, traumas or disappointments. It's a matter of aligning to sound virtues that will help to support and sustain meaningful connection. It's the constant, consistent and compassionate work of preparing the land as fertile ground, etc.

Some relationship influencers often suggest timelines and timeframes for progressing to various stages of a relationship. Truth is that some people have been in relationships for a long time and still aren't "ready." Some people have been abstinent for a while, but still aren't ready. Some people have taken time to heal from their past relationship, but still aren't ready. Some have taken time to build themselves, but still aren't ready to be an active part of supporting and building with another. Some have taken so much time to build themselves that they have built forts no one can penetrate. Time is a great incorporation, but time alone doesn't necessarily heal, fix or make us ready. I mean really, the clock keeps running even when we are running late. Time will tell you to get ready and give you a gauge for deadlines and how many more minutes you have to get ready, but it does not actually wash your tail, dress you and push you out the door.

The real framework for relational progression is widely and wisely based on maturing in alignment to Love and its accompanying principles that not only function in you, but also from you. Ah, and I'll throw this in for free. It's wisely based on maturing in alignment to Love that functions AS YOU!

Again, finding the "right" person is more about readiness than romance. It's about maturity. Being eager is not the same as being ready. True relational compatibility isn't necessarily about who serves your romantic ego. It's really about collaborating in maturity with the spirit of your being and theirs.

There is a deep need for alignment in Love and a clear understanding as well as functioning of its essence. Again ... again, I am not talking about love as mere feelings we have for another; I am speaking about the divine Love that is the essence, spiritual intelligence, wisdom, spirit guided force and unconditional nature at our core. I am talking about the part of us that makes us most like the Creator, the Source, God!

In my previous book, Relationality, I briefly mentioned that romance in the driver's seat of partnership can potentially be dangerous. It's like driving under the influence. Now, don't get me wrong, there is nothing wrong with romance in and of itself. Otherwise, there wouldn't even be a purpose for writing this book. What I am really getting at is that romance can be a manifestation of the greater Love, it is not the fullness of it that will be needed to truly sustain the relationship and fulfill the soul's purpose.

Romance driving the relationship will take you to some exciting places. Some that you will never forget. Also, some you might not even remember because someone slipped you that ecstasy (take that how you want to). You see, romance is generally highly based and driving by fantasy, desires, and the feel-good drug. While this can be beautiful, it will not sustain the relationship when and if the romance happens to fade for a while. So, get your romance on, but don't let it drive the car ... at least not alone or without the supervision of the greater Love.

When the greater Love is the chauffeur, dating and partnership becomes a matter of executing the plans at each place Love brings us to. Romance is then dependent on Love, instead of Love being dependent on romance. The collaboration between the two can yield better results for our soul this way. Please understand, that while I am saying the greater Love is, the greater Love, I am not saying that is belittles romantic Love. I am simply suggesting that it pours the necessary nutrients into romance, because that's what Love does. It causes things to thrive, grow, shine, balance out, etc. Love in essence has a relationship with the other things that color our lives and cultivate our partnering. Hopefully that makes sense to you. If it doesn't, then call me, we can get our coloring books out and sort through it (smile).

In the meantime, I hope you will take time to ponder a bit differently than most. Many people are set on landing the relationship of their dreams. What would happen if instead, you set your heart mind toward landing the relationship of your awakening – as the land itself for which great relationships happen?

CHAPTER 8

THE BENEDICTION

I truly do see you as the land where great relationships can happen. I see in you the essence of our Creator. I see in you the pure light of Love, joy and peace. For some of you, it requires that I look a bit deeper, because I have to get past your stoned faced and the rolling of your eyes for me just saying that (smile), but nonetheless, I see you!

As we conclude this conversation, I want to just remind you that as you go, you have to remember that the true journey of Love is ultimately the discovery of oneness. It is realizing that life itself is a relationship that is evolving in greater awareness of our oneness with the Creator and one another. Our relationships are not about dominating one another, but instead about using the authority in dominion to align and bring balance to it all. In this balancing, please be reminded that it's not about weight, it's about willingness. It's not about who possesses the most, it's about how we collaborate in what we have. It's not about lording over one another, it's about reigning in leadership with one another.

Don't forget, that no one is without error. We must wisely embrace the idea that there will be some hiccups in our relationships ... potentially some major ones. In many cases these hiccups may not be a matter of a lacking in Love, but instead just a mere instance of fear peeking its head. Remember, it's most likely a fear that will require partnering in Love to cast out. You cannot expect to be relationship ready if you are unwilling to be faced with your partner or potential partner's fears, and their responses to fear. This does not mean that you have to live subjected to those fears, but ultimately you must face those fears in partnership with them as a team.

Don't lose sight that life together isn't a matter of forcing your way and rights. Setting boundaries aren't as much about keeping people out as they are about assuming responsibility for yourself and keeping that land cultivated so that your aligned personally and as a well-sourced garden in which others can partake. Partnering shouldn't be a power struggle between egos. It should be a power distribution of and as your authentic self. Working together to overcome any dividing principalities seeking to infiltrate and ruin your connection, closeness, compassion, consideration and cause for one another.

Being relationship ready takes consideration on many ends. You have to ask yourself some questions that are not intended to be disempowering, but instead intended to motivate and give you the wheel. How will you consider your partner socially, emotionally, spiritually, sexually, financially, domestically, etc.? Being relationship ready, means you are moving from me... to *we*. It means you are having to consider someone in things you usually only considered for yourself. This could be challenging in some regard because we have many things that we feel aren't doing any harm to anyone else because hey, we do it by ourselves. Well, even in those scenarios, there are times when you must keep in the forefront of your mind that you are partnered or seeking to partner. This may mean having to put some things down that you normally didn't think twice about picking up. It might mean making the extra effort to turn the porn off because you don't want to bring potentially misinformed or unaligned energy to your bedroom experiences with your partner; causing you to miss them because the images in your head are on screen. It might mean not being able to smoke in the house because your partner can't handle the smoke. It might include being mindful of the DM on social media because some messages can be taken the wrong way or offensively if viewed without understanding from your mate. It might mean finally having to deal with some of the traumas that have been put on the backburner for dealing with since you were comfortable shelving or silencing them. If you are like me, hopefully it doesn't mean you will have to be burdened with the task of having to say good morning when you wake up in the morning (this is an inside joke regarding my relationship). These may be menial things or not applicable to you and your situations, but I think you get the overall point. You have to be considerate, compassionate and in full recognition that you are preparing for or in covenant with another.

As a matter of fact, those 3C's are some good focus points as a relationship ready person. Consideration, Compassion, Covenant. Can you think of some other ones (not necessarily C words) that you can put in your view to aid in your readiness? Truth is, this is serious business. It is very serious and sacred; however that doesn't mean it has to be void of sensuality, surprises, spontaneity, and amusement (ok, I know the A throws off the alliteration, but I couldn't think of an S word for fun, exciting, etc., leave me alone.).

The point is you are capable of having a deeply fulfilling relationship. One that you are not just eager for, but one that you are truly ready for. No, ready doesn't mean you know exactly what will happen (or not happen). It doesn't mean you will not be punched in the gut with some matters of life happening between you and your boo, bae, beau and beauty. More than anything, it means you are aligned and continually aligning yourself to be Love for your significant other. It means you are manifesting as your most authentic self and willing to advance in that as you go about your relationship. It means you are willing to overcome, willing to heal, willing to nurse, willing to support, willing to be your authentic self and allow your partner all the same.

While I don't know in detail what will happen for you or to you in your relationship ready status, I do know that if you embrace and embody wisdom, light and Love, something in your will find a sense of fulfillment and joy that is second to none. Be reminded that this is not a mere pursuit of happiness, it is to be an excursion, exploration and expression of wholeness. It is as simple as understanding the difference between wholeness as a passenger of happiness versus happiness as a passenger of wholeness. If happiness is the primary pursuit, unhappy seasons in the relationship will drive them to swift endings and fragility. When wholeness is the greater value, that wholeness can birth a relationship that brings you something more solid and consistent than happiness – it can bring you divine joy.

I titled this closing chapter's conversation The Benediction because I miss being at church (smile)! No, seriously, I titled it this because I want you to know that everything I am saying here is intended to be an utterance and bestowing of blessing upon you as you move forward in your alignment, pursuit, refreshing or rehab of your relationship. I decree and declare that you will move deeper toward the #iAmLove4u wisdom. You are especially worth it in your distribution and receiving. Again, I see you and know that as you embody relational wisdom, you too will see your partner in a divine way!

As you move forward from the #relationshipgoals and deeper into the reality and wisdom of being relationship ready, it is my sincere hope and prayer that you will manifest as the highest version of your divine self and be partnered with someone that has aligned in being the same.

R elati☸nship EADY

Reflective Visioning Exercises Quick Sheets

*(Full Workshops Facilitated by LeAnzar Stockley available.
Visit www.leanzarstockley.com for more information)*

Use the following quick sheet pages as a guide for reflective introspection and initiative toward establishing your relational philosophy, relationship vision, and enhancement of your relational greatness.

The Reflective Process of Relational Greatness

Relational greatness is about aligning yourself to virtues that are reflective of your inner worth. This is possible to those who are willing to look within themselves and identify the things that contribute to their overall relational prowess. Use this worksheet to initiate reflection and introspection in moving toward meaningful alignment.

What relational elements have you learned from the influencers (parents, friends, media, etc.) in your life?

_____

_____

_____

How would you describe the relationship you want?

_____

_____

_____

What are the things hindering you or posing as obstacles in having the relationship you desire?

_____

_____

_____

What are some specific things you can work on that will move you toward being prepared for a great relationship?

_____

_____

_____

The Relational Philosophy for Relational Greatness

Your relational philosophy is the key wisdom you employ, engage and embody to establish how you operate in relationships. Being aware of this and developing it this in a healthy way will help to clothed you with virtues necessary for contributing your authentic self as the land and producer for great relationships.

After careful thought and consideration, write out the details of your relational philosophy based on the R.E.A.D.Y. acronym. While the "R" represents the overall relational philosophy, for worksheet purposes we will focus it on the Reason for relationships.

R. (reason)

_____

_____

_____

E. (Empathy)

_____

_____

_____

A. (Accountability)

_____

_____

_____

D. (Devotion)

_____

_____

_____

Y. (Yielding)

_____

_____

_____

Write your relational philosophy as a phrase, sentence or paragraph.

_____

_____

_____

Remember, the word philosophy is from the Greek words philein sophia which translates as lover of wisdom. Be sure that your relational philosophy is one that marks you as not just a lover of wisdom, but more importantly – a wise Lover.

The Relationship Vision

Having a clear relationship vision is helpful in intentionally activating your direction, steps, focus and faith for your relationship. Visions can be individual, however if you plan is to be in a relationship, it is important to share and collaborate your vision with your partner. If you are currently single, you can complete this alone; however, if you are currently in a relationship, please take time to complete this with your significant other.

Write as many details as you can based on your relational philosophy and desire for your relationship. Include as many areas of the relationship as you can. Remember to be reasonable, positive, meaningful and keep it all in present tense.

Ex. "We relate in ways that are considerate of one another's emotional, physical and spiritual wellbeing when faced with any posing conflict."

_____
_____
_____
_____
_____
_____
_____
_____
_____
_____
_____
_____
_____
_____
_____
_____
_____
_____
_____
_____
_____
_____

ACKNOWLEDGMENTS

Back in the 1900's we used to give shout outs to people. So, in keeping with that old time loving, I want to give a few shout outs to some key relationships that have helped to make this book a possibility and reality for completion and distribution.

Shout out to Deneishia "Dee" Jacobpito of The Chrystal Stage for the editing work. Not every editor makes room for the artistic voice of the author. Dee was careful to welcome my vernacular shenanigans and personal vocabulary in this book, while keeping me from sounding like I've only graduated from kindergarten. She has generously availed herself and services to me in ways that truly do not go unnoticed or unappreciated.

Shout out to Christopher "Chris Michael" Sherrod for his input on the cover concept for this project. What a difference another set of ideas make. Friend doesn't just get me chicken and 7UP when things aren't going the best, but he also avails himself to mock things up when needed. He'll also punch a few people if I need him to. Now that is relationship right there!

Shout out to Anthony "Tony" Hunter of A. Eric Group for his unrestricted help on multiple fronts of this project, from formatting, spiritual, verbal and tangible encouragement in making this all a manifest reality. Having the type of support that goes beyond words, means the world to me. Tony has delivered such support.

Last but not least, shout out to my guy, the Beau himself, Rashian Boyd. Putting up with the rambling and scrambling of all it took to get this book done, fell directly on Shian's ear. I am sure that now that this book is complete, he doesn't even want to hear the words Relationship READY ever again in life. But ... oh well, he will. The support and Love given during this process is nothing shy of suitable. The input from everyday conversation to the frustration of exactly how to present this book hasn't been the easiest, but Shian's support has not faltered. Maybe he is on the verge of being truly Relationship READY (LOL)!

MEET MR. RELATIONALITY

Author, Speaker and Relationality Specialist. LeAnzar "Zar" Stockley is the founder of Into God Network and Soulciety61 Collaborative Alliance for Relational Wellness.

As a Relationality Specialist, Ordained Minister, Workshop Clinician and lifelong student of human relationships, he is devoted to supporting relational wellness through expanded consciousness in spiritual intelligence and the relational wisdom in personal, ministry and business relationships.

Zar facilitates as a compassionate spiritual practitioner, accompanying individuals on their journey of alignment in being their authentic selves and contributors to fulfilling relationships.

He holds a Master of Arts in Human Services Counseling: Marriage & Family, undergrad degrees in Psychology & Christian Counseling and Worship Studies, Advanced Diploma in Biblical Counseling, certification as a life coach, relationship workshop facilitator, and mindfulness coach. He is also a certified Prepare-Enrich Facilitator, Licensed Marriage Officiant, and Effective Black Parenting Training Instructor.

More Titles From This Author

Identity ChRISt.IS
ISBN: 978-1934937-82-2

Relationality:
Consciously Aligning to Our Divine Relational Worth

ISBN: 978-1-5127-9031-3 (sc)
ISBN: 978-1-5127-9031-3 (hc)
ISBN: 978-1-5127-9031-3 (e)

To Contact LeAnzar Stockley for Speaking Events, Workshops,
Retreats, One to One and Group Sessions or to find out more
about services provided, visit

SOULCIETY61
Collaborative Alliance for Relational Wellness
Las Vegas, Nevada
zar@leanzarstockley.com
www.leanzarstockley.com